T0065226

NOW HERE

NOW HERE

A SOUL'S JOURNEY

ELLE ELLSWORTH

Archway Publishing books may be ordered through booksellers or by contacting:

Archway Publishing
1663 Liberty Drive
Bloomington, IN 47403
www.archwaypublishing.com
844-669-3957

Scripture quotations marked KJV are from the Holy Bible, King James Version
(Authorized Version). First published in 1611. Quoted from the KJV Classic
Reference Bible, Copyright © 1983 by The Zondervan Corporation.

ISBN: 978-1-6657-5154-4 (sc)
ISBN: 978-1-6657-5155-1 (e)

Library of Congress Control Number: 2023919457

Print information available on the last page.

Archway Publishing rev. date: 10/18/2023

CONTENTS

Part 4: Do Due Diligence

ACKNOWLEDGEMENTS

This book would not have been possible had it not been for those who provided a roadmap to follow and one having a mindset to follow that path. There are so many great men and women who have impacted my life experience one way or another. I will attempt to share with you what that impact looks like. First, I would like to thank God for entrusting me with his purpose. He inspired me throughout this writing with words and thought ideas that only he could put together. I was guided during each stage of this process and when I asked questions, the next step was there in front of me. I could not have planned a better outline.

The next step consisted of listening to those who have traveled this path before me and gleaning as much knowledge as possible. Many of the resources available were not useful; however, I did find a lot of reputable resources and tools that I use today. So do your research. The list below provides a few resources I found useful one way or another. As a disclaimer, I am not being paid to promote any of the below listed resources; they are listed for research purposes only.

Words cannot express my humility, thankfulness, gratitude, and joy for experiencing the most valuable Source of ALL, my God, the Living One, the Holy Grail within, embracing me in PURE LOVE. This was my chief aim and purpose; to discover my purpose for coming to this plane of existence. Special thanks to the following Spiritual Teachers and Leaders, Authors, Philosophers, Poets, YouTube Channels, Apps, and Movies.

- The Holy Bible (KJV)
- Theodore Nottingham (Gospel of Thomas)
- Dr. Elaine Pagels (Gospel of Thomas)
- Dr. Mike Heiser
- Dr. Wayne Dyer
- Neville Goddard
- Neale Donald Walsh
- William Walker Atkinson
- Dr. Joe Dispensa
- Napoleon Hill
- Dr. Joseph Murphy
- Oprah Winfrey
- Dr. Panjesh Naram (Master Healer)
- Dr. Clint Rogers (Ancient Secrets of a Master Healer)
- Andrew Wommack
- Manifest App (App Store)
- Law of Attraction App (App Store)

Pay close attention to these varied resources. They are as opposing as one could ever imagine. But one thing is clear, the above resources share a common theme, which all point to the same truth. You can find the above resources on You Tube or go to the author's website. I am incredibly grateful for the free resources that proved to be invaluable. I cannot tell you the number of times I've listened to these audio/video recordings. The Apps were especially useful to aid in organizing a schedule for setting aside quiet time for putting in the work. Some of these resources continue to serve as a tool for further study and review on my unending journey. It is critical to maintain consistency and a positive mindset. I cannot say this enough.

Developing a daily routine is vital to retraining your brain to focus on whatsoever things are true, whatsoever things are honest, whatsoever things are just, whatsoever things are pure, whatsoever things are lovely, whatsoever things are of good report; if there be any virtue, and if there be any praise, think on these things (Phil 4:8, KJV). Once you have developed a habit of retraining your mind, you may find repetitive work mundane. If this occurs, follow your intuition as you will know from within how to continue your journey.

SPECIAL NOTE TO THE READERS

While reading this book, keep in mind that we are no different in the eyes of God because all he sees is our wonderful and beautiful soul, which is a part of Himself. I ask further, while reading, imagine that this is *your* GOD talking with you about *you*. This bears repeating... just imagine that this is *your* GOD talking with *you* about YOU. If you do this one thing while reading this book, your life will never be the same.

PREFACE
(NOTE FROM THE AUTHOR)

This book is nothing more than a recollection of LIFE events and EXPERIENCES I chose to share with all of you, in the hope that you may begin to remember who you really are. I am one of many enlisted by GOD to share this because it is the masses who are "sleep-living" and don't know that they are "sleep-living." Sleep-living is like the walking dead.

Our existence as we know it is gradually slipping away from us because we are destroying our world and ourselves; and if we fail to change course, we will destroy our planet. We have a lot of work to do on a collective conscious level, and collectively, we can do it. There're already so many other precious souls who have stepped into their role of awareness and are doing their life's work. While others will continue to play their role in this earthly realm, until they choose a different role that is better suited to fulfil a higher purpose for the mutual benefit of all.

This shift in collective consciousness is not something that can be mandated or legislated. It must be a personal choice to desire a better state of being not only for yourself; but for everyone, as we are all connected; therefore, whatever affects you and I, affects us ALL.

I've come to know that this journey IS LIFE, itself, a process unfolding before your very eyes; but you must open your heart to allow connection to your Source of LIFE, whether that's your

God, your Allah, your Brahman, your Vishnu, your Buddha, your Whatever… so that you may come to KNOW and EXPERIENCE that which you really are in this Relative Realm.

And now after having EXPERIENCED what and who I really AM, I cannot help but be anxious to share this good news with you. When deciding to adopt a different perspective than the one that is currently viewed, we become open to hear with our hearts and CHANGE the WORLD. It begins with each of us becoming aware of our existence and surroundings, seeing it for what it is and connecting it with the sustaining life that Earth provides for us ALL. This life sustaining energy flows in and through all of us, individually and collectively.

Having a better understanding of humankind's existence or come to KNOW, EXPERIENCE, and now BEING, a new creature in Christ, did not occur in a building known as the "church." Don't get it twisted…I condemn not the church; I am merely stating that truth must be EXPERIENCED, and this can happen anywhere, anytime. David said if I go to the bottom of the ocean, God is there. Each EXPERIENCE may be different for each of us and may also look different. God cannot be defined nor can be ruled out as undefined. The scripture in the book of I Corinthians, chapter two comes to mind…

> 11For who among men knows the thoughts of man except his own spirit within him? So too, no one knows the thoughts of God except the Spirit of God. 12We have not received the spirit of the world, but the Spirit who is from God, that we may understand what God has freely given us.[1]

I am no one…just a tiny little voice crying in a wasteland to remind you of something…" Jesus has already come in the flesh, and

---

[1] https://biblehub.com/1_corinthians/2-11.htm

Spirit." John wrote to prepare us of Jesus' coming; but I tell you Jesus has come and demonstrated to us how to exercise the power within in this physical realm. And so did all the other Masters and spiritual leaders across this Universe. They knew of and EXPERIENCED this power … that is the power of the Gospel of Good News. But here in the Western world, we have lost sight of those things that truly do move mountains. Nothing on a global scale is going to change until we collectively come together and affect the change we desire. Newsflash!!! God isn't going to do anything until we do something about our state of being. He has freely given us everything we need to make this happen and is waiting to aid us in the process of creating…it's all about a collective mindset focused on the mutual benefit of ALL.

Stop and take a look around; the state of being for the majority of us is not as we would like. Other forms of worldly rulers, governments, and organized religions who do not allow one to think for oneself, and of course worldly government and politics, all have and play their major roles well. These are the mountains that we face and the same mountains that must be built on a solid foundation and not on sinking sand or should I say, and not from decisions made from a place of strategic guessing. Everybody takes chances with human lives every day all day, nonstop, from all aspects of LIFE. This has to stop!

This is the value that is placed on LIFE….. ah God…. ah Life…. did I say God? THINK about this! What would be the difference? God being ALL in ALL and through ALL. We view God in ways that are familiar to us and if and when He appears different from the times of old, we dismiss the premise that this could very well be God. When God shows up different than what we are accustomed, we miss God on so many levels. Open UP! "Can't confine God no matter how you try." God is in and through *all* that exists and can be found in the means we use to try and confine him. We tend to limit and confine or restrict God. We must stop doing this!

Does having a mindset of restriction and limitation, when it comes to God, add to our current state of existence? We all played a role in creating this world and continue to do so. Now is the time to decide whether you like your role, or you choose to evolve into a higher role for the mutual benefit of ALL…. Only you know how to play your role and no one else can tell you how… Once you open up and face yourself (the good, the bad, and the ugly) … it's over! You no longer depend on others to orchestrate your life or tell you how to EXPERIENCE LIFE (GOD); you are now in control from a space of EXPERIENCING the power and the wisdom (Jesus) of GOD. Operating from a space of higher consciousness can begin a process to create an even greater shift in restoring our temporary home, Earth, and all its beauty.

We need to wake up, come to our senses, and come home to Father, just as the Prodigal Son after experiencing life in this physical world of "sleep-living." After doing things his way, all he had was a big heap of dung in the pigpen (creation by default instead of creation from a state of awareness). But he woke up, just as I did, and I hope many of you. It is my sincere desire, you realized your state of being, and if it's not to your pleasing, open up…. And watch what happens!

The Father saw his Son afar off, and met him with outstretched arms, to greet him, before he made it home…. Father wanted his son to know… "I see YOU! It brings me great pleasure to see my child coming home." This is so beautiful to me …He saw me then, and He sees YOU now, regardless of your state of being.

Enter your secret closet in private and talk to yourself or God… either way it sounds ludicrous, but that's a key to life in this physical relative plane. He stands at the door knocking, just waiting for you to enter your secret closet and lock the door behind you to let Him in. He has been waiting for you all your life to tell you how wonderful you are and from whence you came and how you came. He longs to share with you the secrets of life and how to experience life on this physical plane. He wants to tell you to enjoy the path that leads to Him. There are nuggets strewn along the way that gives you joy unspeakable and your cup runneth over.

This kind of blows a lot of dogma out the window... but remember to build a solid foundation and that's what scripture did for me and continues to do so. I am able to interpret scripture with more accuracy NOW than before my EXPERIENCE. But remember, this is what I found to be my truth. It may also be your truth; but not necessarily. It is absolute that GOD IS ALL THERE IS and IS NOT. A whole other aspect of God's divinity.

Which leads me to this. We have attributed so many things as something God says or scripture says, we've lost sight of the fact that we truly are spiritual beings first and foremost, residing in this physical body (restrictive form) encased by our individual soul and most importantly, all wrapped up by the soul of GOD. God has me covered and I have come to know and accept this as my truth, and I EXPERIENCED this KNOWING. You must come to KNOW and EXPERIENCE your truth for yourself. It's being born again and becoming a NEW creature.

At the time I began what I thought was my journey, I was embarking in LIFE on a well-defined path. I had no concept of where *LIFE* would lead; but I kept seeking and seeking; and I continued to seek looking for truth in whatever form that resonated with me. I have come to trust what God brings to me as pure because it always aligns with Love, Joy, and Truth. No one can convince me otherwise that what I AM now REMEMBERING, and EXPERIENCING is not GOD.

My sole intention when I became serious about life and this so-called journey, was to change my life because I knew life had more to offer; and so, I had to find out. I tried to find answers in different churches of various denominations, but I found it hard to look past my conscious mind at what goes on inside the church. Nevertheless, I understand LIFE much better NOW. And why things are the way they are. People need to be aware of who they are inside and outside the church. Awareness is key to experiencing the power of God.

As I was saying, I began with one intention and that was change and God knew all that this "change" consisted of; So, He told me to start with Matthew 6:33, "Seek ye first the kingdom of God and His righteousness, and all these things shall be added unto you." And I did just that.

It began around the end October 2021 when I became consistent in journaling. After being in lockdown nearly two years, I had a lot of time to really reflect on LIFE (GOD) and the question I asked is this, "what must I do to enjoy a state of well-being and all it consist, on this side?" I yearned to know.

I ached inside to change my state of being to one more suited to who I knew I really AM deep down but lack the knowledge as to how to unlock what many call the hidden secrets to LIFE; And so, it began as I sat and wrote freestyle...whatever came to mind; and before I knew it, I was journaling every day. This became my routine and I found journaling quite rewarding and fulfilling. I looked forward to these special times where I EXPERIENCED the embrace of PURE LOVE.

Then I noticed my writing was taking its own shape or form so to speak, like a portrait coming to life on a canvas. As I continued seeking, God would lead me to information that either answered a question or led me to another truth. Then pieces of information begin to fit perfectly together that helped me understand the questions I have regarding the Bible, and how it came to be the canonized Bible we use today. Then, I began to notice a slight paradigm shift, it is this shift that propelled me to continue... and so, I continued seeking and seeking... having one EXPERIENCE after another ...and before I knew it...I AM.... NOW HERE.

INTRODUCTION

Did you ever stop and wonder about the things you see with your natural eye and how they came into existence, or should I say "being"? Well, I have… and not only just my surroundings and environment, but I wondered when and how did it all begin. All I know is that I showed up in a world that was already here. So again, I asked how all this stuff we see get here.

Now, I'm not talking about all the tall buildings and beautiful edifices; but what I am talking about is the wind we feel gently across our face, the designated big oceans and their precise locations, the flames of fire dancing randomly, and rain falling from the sky but only in certain areas…. all these things that seem so common to us today. Even when you stop and observe nature as the wind rustles the fall leaves or you see dust in a whirlwind, or even the worker ants busy at work; for me this is the awe of nature and I know there must be an enormous powerful force that is responsible for such mind-blowing scenes.

Now, I want you to get into the moment and become aware of your being. One may ask how do you do this? Some of you may be saying…" Here we go again, another one of "those" books! Not exactly! Some of the material in this book may be old to some and new to others; however, my goal is to explain our "connectedness" and paint a new portrait of who we really are and how we are interconnected.

This book is not intended to be treated as dogma. Furthermore, it is not intended to be used as a manual in the sense of "how tos". This book is a journey of realization from a very practical point of view and is to be used as such. This is what worked in a time frame that adjusted to the level and duration of personal commitment. Each journey is different and your commitment to your journey determines how long it will take to effect a change in your life. It doesn't have to take years to realize your truth.

Thank you for taking time to stop and smell the roses. It is my sincere desire that something said in this book ignites a fire within to seek for yourself to prove to yourself, that you were right all along. That is the least one can do to discover how beautiful and wonderful life can be and is supposed to be. So much has clouded our worldview and belief system that make it almost impossible for one to shift to a different mindset.

If you are reading this book and have a yearning to know how to unlock the secret to fulfill your life experience and positively impact others, then you should consider reading this book in its entirety. Additionally, if you are determined to find the answer to life's questions and create the life you want for yourself, family, and generations to come, congratulations, you have found a great book to get started.

Regardless of your background, faith, ethnicity, etc....there is something in this book you can implement immediately to begin a process to change your life. You must believe that change is happening when you do not see change. It's a <u>knowing</u>! This book is not based on New Age dogma. It's based on a journey to find purpose; and as research led to different sources, the Law of Attraction initially stood out. Research revealed the Laws of the Universe were created by God Almighty and there is nothing New Age about this. In fact, it's Old Age.

This book will reveal a process to transform your mindset and inevitably your life. You won't have to jump through hoops or invest a lot of money. You already have everything you need to begin your journey…YOU. Other tangible resources (phone, computer, etc.… to access to internet), pen, paper, and this book, is all you need to begin. Having access to other online resources will aid you on your journey; however, the tangible essentials to begin starts with YOU. You must be ready for change and willing to do what it takes to effect change in your life.

Within humankind (that's us) is the essence of God, Emmanuel, Light, Spirit, Source, Mother Earth, Universe, whatever is familiar to you …faith of a mustard seed, to ignite a force so powerful, it goes thermonuclear…you get the idea. The other listed tangible items go hand in hand.

What all of this come down to is you must be willing to invest time in silence to hear yourself think. Otherwise, transformation is a fleeting thought blown away by the wind of your busy thought life. Herman Melville (born August 1, 1819, New York City—died September 28, 1891, New York City), an American novelist, short-story writer, and poet, best known for his novels of the sea, including his **masterpiece, Moby Dick (1851)** said, "God's one and only voice is silence[2]." The Bible says this even better, "Be still and know that I AM God" (Ps 46:10, KJV).

Again, this book is meant to be an easy read and very practical. It is also being written while life experiences are transforming into new creations. You are as much a part of this magnificent experience as anyone because you are the reason this book is being written.

---

[2] https://quotefancy.com/quote/1006518/Herman-Melville-God-s-one-and-only-voice-is-silence

PART I

WELCOME TO EARTH, YOUR NEW HOME

CHAPTER ONE

OUTRAGEOUS RIGHT (RELIGION AND SCIENCE MEET)

Did you ever stop and wonder, "what is this stuff I'm made of"? I'm talking about the human body's composition, down to the smallest atom. The human body and all its parts and systems, has the ability to heal itself; as well as automatic cell regeneration up to every eleven months,[3] is nothing short of miraculous And if this is not amazing enough, think about the intelligence and order of all the systems working in sync, for the mutual benefit of a well-functioning physical body.

There must be something within this miraculous form, known as the "body" that keep it functioning and operating in rhythm. In school, we learned in Biology, most of the parts of the body and how they are designed to work together to provide a glimpse of divine order at work. Our bodies are amazing human physical forms and is made up of physical matter and spiritual essence. To paraphrase the Bible, we are beautifully and wondrously made, that is in GOD's image with all God's attributes (Gen 1:26-28, KJV).

Now let's get back to the smallest unit. In school, we also learned about the atom (electron, protons, neutrons), molecules, etc..... What

---

[3] https://www.scientificamerican.com/article/our-bodies-replace-billions-of-cells-every-day/

do you think will happen if that smallest unit continues to get smaller and smaller? No matter how many times you split the atom, it will continue to split into infinity. Welcome to Quantum Theory (Physics and Mechanics)[4]. This theory has been in existence since the dawn of Creation; however, only within the past few centuries have scientists come to get a glimpse of this new universe so to speak.

One scientist in particular Albert Einstein, who is known as one of the greatest scientists of all time and is credited with mathematically proving the movement of invisible particles dancing (motion).[5] The fundamental principle that everything consists of atoms and is constantly in motion. This is an important reality to conceptualize. I strongly suggest researching this theory for yourself to gain a deeper understanding of how this theory operates, so that you can grasp some concept of how this strange science impacted mankind in the primordial beginning (Gen 1:3, KJV). GOD is Love; Love is the most powerful emotion there is and has its own vibration; therefore GOD is the vibration of Love. Everything you see has its own vibration... And this includes humankind…you and I. Now, if you think about it, this goes hand in hand with scripture… God is spirit (John. 6:63, KJV), which can be compared to a form of energy, which has its own vibration (movement). All of this is connected whether we agree or not.

This is a fascinating area of study, and more people are developing an interest as a novice seeker, such as myself. Please be patient for the next several pages as an attempt to explain in plain and simple language, how Quantum Physics changed my worldview about how

---

[4] https://www.amnh.org/exhibitions/einstein/legacy/quantum-theory

[5] https://www.ans.org/news/article-969/albert-einstein-and-the-most-elemental-atomic-theory/#:~:text=Einstein%20also%20in%201905%20mathematically,use%20of%20statistics%20and%20probability.&text=Atomic%20theory%20says%20that%20any,always%20in%20random%2C%20ceaseless%20motion.

I came into being. But first before I explain this linkage, you must understand a little bit about me.

I was born and raised in a small rural town in Mississippi. I lived with my grandmother who was widowed and raising three older children of her own. My mother died when I was around six and my paternal grandmother reared my younger brother and I. We grew up poor, but we managed to survive the cold icy winters. I remember seeing ice cycles six feet long, hanging from huge trees and houses. During the long cold winter months, the scenery looked just like a greeting card straight out of a box of Hallmark Christmas cards.

My grandmother ensured we went to church at least twice a month. Of course, we only had service twice a month. Our church had a very small congregation. At best, the most in attendance on either of the twice-a-month services would be no more than about fifteen people, including children. The church was small and about five miles from where we lived, and for a time, we would walk to church, and someone would be kind enough to drive us back home. Then after about a couple of years or so, one of my uncles bought a car and finally, no more walking.

Growing up as a Missionary Baptist Christian, we lived by doctrine…living by the letter, instead of by the Spirit. I remembered, when I was about eight years old, I was always reading either a book or the Bible and my grandmother would always question me about my studious attitude and would say, "why you study so hard…. must be a professor" or something to that effect. She lived to be over 100 years young before transitioning in 2014.

I am grateful she spoke life into me about my attitude, although, at the time, it was meant as sarcasm. What she said became more imbedded in my being; and I became more determined to be the best at whatever I endeavored. I took what she said very seriously. And having that kind of mindset at such an early age, I believe set the stage for the path life would eventually lead.

I graduated high school at sixteen in 1975, top of my class

and granted full academic scholarship to Alcorn State University, Lorman, MS. I found myself in a world I had no idea where or how I would fit. Luckily, I managed to find work in a Work Study program, working for my college advisor performing light house cleaning, laundry, and ironing. It was easy work and kept spending money in my pocket. As I look back, my college years are just a mere blur. Although I enrolled in five to six classes each semester, I participated in sports and other extracurricular activities. I also played basketball during my freshman year. Believe it or not, I played basketball during my junior and high school years and was very good.

After I left college, I began to experience life truly on my own so to speak. I had no idea what to expect. But somehow, I managed to find my way. The one common thread during my newfound independence, I knew deep within my being, this life seemingly appeared somehow surreal to me; but I ignored what my inner man was telling me. This inner knowing is the soft nudge by GOD, letting you know you I'm HERE. This deep knowing is what has sustained me in very difficult times during my early young adulthood.

Several years had gone by and I'm now in my early twenties, working in a state position. I thought, "I'm on my way now that I have a 'good job with benefits', decent social relationships, and a contentment with life to some degree".

As I grew older, not necessarily wiser, I could FEEL something gnawing at me; still uncertain as to how to identify this feeling, that was always present with me, I always knew there was more to what was obvious deep within. Sometimes, though we tend to forget that this inner presence is with us. because we become so engulfed with life and too busy to recognize when you live in a state of being what I refer to as "sleep-living"; then, we find ourselves existing in a world that appears as a maze with no exit. It's time to wake up and get out of the maze. It's time to stop living your past repeatedly.

Now, life is beginning to take form, and circumstances and

events are occurring that are wreaking havoc in my life. You become so excited about your life now that you have what many of us referred to as a good job or career, becoming a member of exclusive organizations, fraternities, private clubs, high profile churches, and so forth and so on; but then life happens and wham, slap right in the face! please, do not misunderstand me, and hear me clearly.

There is absolutely nothing wrong with these desires and privileges; furthermore, this is NOT my point. My point is how these things distract us from spending time alone to get to know the real SELF who is seldom heard from or visited. If change is desired, spending time alone is a must. You must have an idea of who you are before you know what changes to effect in your life. To put it simply, you must recognize there IS something unsatisfying about your life and wellbeing and feel compelled to do something about what you no longer wish to experience in your life.

Back to the story...it has been a generation or two now and life is really starting to shape into something I'd later find out, invaluable. I didn't know at the time how life's choices shape the physical world we live in today. As I mentioned, choices were made that depleted nearly every ounce of positive energy from my body and surroundings. This lack of positive energy developed into stagnation and my body became the breeding ground for all sorts of underlying maladies to take root. I had no concept of the magnitude of the *thought world* and how the Mind of Consciousness impacts our physical world.

It was during this time, I began yearning for my biological mother, whom I had never known in the physical realm. I made choices in my life that were regretful, and I needed someone I trusted from the depth of my soul to talk to, and I had no one. It was during this time I began to do some "soul searching" and realized (came to my senses-Prodigal Son) I always have someone to talk to. Someone who listens to me and does not just hear what I say, someone who can lead me on the path of righteousness for his name's sake. Despite what others may say about "the" path. I am confident I am on my chosen path.

When this resonated with me, more precious seeds were planted. I had what I thought were friends, but I never felt comfortable sharing my deep thoughts. I had one very special friend in high school and early years of college; but overtime, we somehow lost touch. I am so thankful and grateful that we reconnected in 2014 and remain in touch to this day.

We often hear stories of how people were miraculously healed, someone landed that dream job, a new young executive made the deal of the century, or someone won the lottery. Have you ever asked the question "how come that don't happen to me"? Well, I have! Maybe not those exact questions, but something very similar. I had read a book called "Hung by the Tongue" during this time and was seeking knowledge to grasp understanding about the world that is not so nice, from where I was sitting (my perspective). This was my first glimpse of self-creation that was not so pretty.

As I started asking questions of myself, I came across another book called the Power of the Subconscious Mind, by Dr. Joseph Murphy, and began reading. I soon realized there is a connection between our physical world and the words we speak, according to this book. As I look back, this was during the mid to late 80's when I had an encounter with this kind of basic knowledge of what IS… there is a cultural saying…"it IS what it IS". We say this lightly, but there is a much greater meaning behind this phrase.

I attended church all my life and had no understanding of the Spirit of God and how HE works, and this connection. I thought I knew; but I did not have a clue. This book, I think, was a seed planted that would grow into something so wonderful. There are no words to express the exhilaration of this journey and the discovery of everything we need is within reach here.

There is another side to the impact this book made in my life. Remember my Christian background, Southern Baptist with a twist of Pentecostal, well this book (Power of Subconscious Mind) was hard to swallow. Although it made all the sense in the world, but because of my Christian teaching, I found myself in a conundrum. I was scared to death, (for effect) to consider what I read in this book, serious enough to begin to study the content. I believed from the depth of my being, if I pursued this knowledge, I would be committing blasphemy against God and the Holy Spirit. And not only was it forbidden; I will go straight to hell if I indulge in such esoteric knowledge.

I believed this kind of knowledge is considered as New Age teaching and anyone who read or study such knowledge is an enemy of God, a messenger of Satan and is damned by God; and will use the Bible to prove it. By the way, this is the Bible Emperor Constantine instituted during the fourth century and is the Bible we use today (More about this later). I was a firm believer in what I was taught by Christian leaders, preachers, and teachers. As a bonus to solidify this mindset, I graduated from Dallas Baptist University, Dallas, TX as cum laude in 2005, earning a BA in Psychology, and a minor in Biblical Studies.

Although, seeds had been planted, it took years for me to recognize I needed to protect the seed. Birds of prey and other earthbound gnawers can dig up the seed, to prevent germination from taking place. Events and circumstances that occur naturally in life are examples of how the seed is dug up. We live day to day unaware of what is taking place in our minds. Before we can see change is needed, we must stop for just a moment, breathe, exhale, and keep quiet. Ask yourself, "what do I need to do to change my life to align with my desires?". You must die to self before you can be reborn into the person you desire to be.

Germination is the process where the seed incubates so that when death occurs, life can burst forth. And so must you! And so must we all! I cannot count the times I allowed my seed to be dug up. So, I kept replanting. I had not yet reached a level of understanding that taught me how to protect my seed. I had reached a stage in my life where I knew I wanted to change my life, but I did not know how or where to begin.

Have you ever had someone tell you, God will work it out! This is one of many cliches spoken when an individual if facing a crisis. They never give you any other information with this proclamation. But this may be enough…it all depends on the vibration you emit… in other words the feeling behind your thoughts about anything.

After reading the book, Power of the Subconscious Mind, I went about life as usual, day to day routines. I became involved in my work and my family. Life seemed good enough I thought, but there was still a void in me that was unfulfilled. It seemed as if life was gradually leaving me and was evident if you could have looked into my eyes.

I heard somewhere, the eyes are the mirror to soul; if this is so, you could see the hurt and pain my soul was experiencing. This is when I began to journal. I believe this too was during the mid to late 80's. Journaling is an excellent form of release, because if there is no one else you can trust, you can trust yourself, when you are ready to open up. Remember, this is where GOD resides.

By now the church is an integral part of my life and I became wrapped up in the performances during service, instead of paying close attention to what was happening despite the performances. I was attending a Pentecostal church now and I thought, surely this is where the presence of God dwells. Emotions ran high during church service and we're on fire for the Lord, as we would say. Well, I lack the understanding about the nature of God, nevertheless, this experience taught me a valuable lesson.

It shouldn't have been a surprise to find just as much control, manipulation, division, strife, and false teaching inside the church as there is outside. My expectations were grounded in scriptural teachings taught throughout my life; and I did expect more, especially those who say they love God and God's children. That soon came to a screeching halt! I met another side of myself I never knew existed.

I became cynical, indignant, indifferent, and most of all disappointed. I somehow felt vindicated for having such strong feelings and did not hesitate to share my negative comments to anyone who would listen. Have you ever known anyone like that? Or better yet, have you ever felt like this? The place I went to seek refuge and spiritual knowledge, is now a place I despise. I could feel my soul aching from even more pain and hurt. Hold up!!! Don't stone me!

I felt lost and alone and sadly enough, I did not know in my conscious mind the extent of God's love for me. There were fleeting moments of a spiritual experience, but it was just that, a fleeting moment. I had trained my mind that this only happens in church. I had no idea I could feel this way all the time. I did not know then as I know now, it doesn't matter about those performances because each of us have a responsibility to focus on becoming the best version of OURselves.

You may be thinking by now, "what does all this have to do with Quantum Theory?" Don't worry, I will get to that and make the connection just as it was revealed to me. GOD created all the laws that govern this Universe or the Cosmos. And Quantum Theory is just one of those areas that is now a topic of interest to many spiritual leaders, theologians, scientists, doctors, historians, and philosophers. I can't tell you how far this expands, but my inner knowing, knows GOD is Infinite. And Quantum Theory as it relates to the world of sciences (neurosciences and physics, along with other forms of research), is mind-boggling. Now some of you may view this as science being in the forefront of something that is astounding; but do not hold the science above its Creator in contempt.

As I pondered the science behind one of my startling revelations, making a connection to the divine Mind and Source, I came to know that this is GOD, whom I call Father and was manifested at the primordial beginning as Light. This powerful Light is the

Creator of ALL, is ALL and through ALL. GOD created the Laws of the Universe. Now whether all the laws governing the universe have been discovered or not is irrelevant. But as *life* continues to evolve, this process of discovery is ongoing. No one can know this, because how can you study GOD's glory to discover new unknown laws? We will never reach the end of any journey embarked upon.

Having a basic knowledge of Quantum Physics' aspect of the Quantum Theory has helped me recognize the energy that is vibrating within me at this very moment is found everywhere. And this same energy vibrates within you too, whether you are aware or not. That is beside the point. Because probability is fundamental to this theory, no wonder science and all its wonders are mind-boggling.

I am an avid listener of various theologians, spiritual leaders, and philosophers and I believe it was Dr. Wayne Dyer who said, "When we change the way we look at things, the things we look at change". Ponder this statement…and consider the possibilities or should I say probabilities. I dare to say they are synonymous in this instance. Now if this premise is true, and I believe it to be so; then, what I see can be significantly different from what another may see. I venture to say the mindset is a key factor in how we perceive the world and the environment that surrounds us.

CHAPTER TWO

NOW THAT I'M HERE

Now that I'm here, now what? "Too much noise I can't hear myself think"! We've all heard this before. Whether it's the kids, riding the bus or rail, on your lunch break, or around other crowded and noisy places, it doesn't matter. Background noise has become so common and a part of our daily lives, it can no longer be heard. It seems our mind has become a mere tool to plan and schedule meetings, the next agenda, how to stay ahead of the competitor, and on and on I could go. Today, planning is on another level.

Now, we must contend with staying safe in the midst of a pandemic. But here's an interesting observation. Think about this... Anytime you drive to a destination and don't remember doing it, is a clear indication of how we can train the mind to control the body unintentionally, just by mere repetition, unknowingly. We trained our mind; but we didn't pay attention to what was taking place behind the scenes of these oblivious moments.

The mind is always engaged in minding other functions on the conscious and unconscious levels; but somehow in the midst of performing all that the mind does, you may create a state of being where one slips away somewhere amid daily consciousness. I don't know about you, but this has happened to me quite a few times. Where did I go? I was operating a vehicle in a robotic state and didn't remember the surrounding traffic until I returned to a state of awareness of what was happening around me on the freeway. And nothing happened, thank GOD!

How did this happen? Think about this scene for just a moment. So much noise going on around us day in and day out. It's a wonder we can finally settle down for a moment just to exhale. Well, maybe not just exhale, but you get the idea. Life happens to all of us and it's up to you to stop and take a mental sabbatical as well as a mental inventory to introduce you to YOURself and connect with what is continuously going on around you.

For some of us, this may be the farthest thing from the conscious mind; however, this is where miracles are created. Driving unaware is a sure sign that my angels were guiding the car. At least that's my explanation. You may choose to think what you like, but I know despite the moments when we are unaware of our conscious actions, I know God was and is in those times when we slip away unaware..

Again, you wonder, "where do I begin" to change my life. Now that you are aware that your life must change, make that commitment to change it. This is when the work begins. The first step of beginning your journey is now underway. Accepting the life that is there before you, is step one. Whether you are living from paycheck to paycheck or living a life you are proud to say you built, it doesn't matter, your thoughts had a huge impact on your lifestyle.

Aligning with this known fact is instrumental before you can move on to the next step. You may proclaim, "I didn't ask for any of this"! take a moment and look back on your life and reflect. Your past and my past reflect our thought-world that reflects the current state of being.

Here is a startling statement…hold on, don't fall off the couch; but, based on my research, the Mind of Consciousness is filled with every thought known to man and is still out there somewhere in the Cosmos. When you have thoughts that align with similar thoughts in the Mind of Consciousness, those thoughts join your thoughts and creates a huge ripple in the Ethereal world and manifests as reality in the physical realm. This can be mind-boggling to say the least. To believe the life that you are experiencing at this very moment, regardless of whether you are in the US or across the globe, is the life that somehow was influenced by thoughts.

I know what some of you may be thinking..." what about the people in Africa and other third world countries...did thoughts influence their life"? and my answer to that question is "Yes"! You must understand that there is a lot of negative energy that has been created and it seeks out its own likeness.

How and why life manifests this way is no different from what is mentioned in the Bible. Despite the opinion of many, everyone has a role to play regardless, and it will be played by someone. The good news is, if you find yourself in a role that is not to your liking, you can evolve in your current role to one aligned with your goals and desires, that benefits humankind.

Once you become familiar with the role you are now playing, ensure to stay in your lane. We love to be in the know and share opinions about every subject that hits the news. Keep in mind, while sharing opinions, there is always a way to reframe a negative response; you must be mindful of your words, which are just as powerful as thoughts. Words are thoughts in action! This is my definition. Don't believe I memorized this from another source. If so, it is not intentional.

It is not our right to think we know what is right or best for someone else. No one can live anyone else's life, so "stay in yo lane bro". As a simple exercise, begin to take mental note when you cross the line, that is, your unsolicited input. Does not matter how simple the matter is. Just start to pay attention and you will be amazed as to how liberating this simple awareness trick works. (See Chapter Four for additional information regarding the roles we play).

Sometimes, it is a struggle to not voice an opinion; but then remember to think before you speak, to be careful about the words you vocalize in response to sensitive issues. We live in an opinionated world therefore it is imperative to stop and think before speaking. Remember, this book is about change, and you must be mindful of not only your thoughts, but behaviors and emotions as well. Repeating the past behaviors will produce your current result; whatever that looks like. You will keep living your past.

Again, one must understand how much negative energy exists in the Mind of Consciousness and recognize when a thought seems to appear out of nowhere, somewhere in the Mind of Consciousness, that thought was attracted to your mindset because you aligned with that specific vibration of energy. This field of Consciousness has been expanding continuously and will continue to expand as we are all thinking human *beings*...

As I wrapped my brain around this incomprehensible concept, I remembered thinking a strange thought, back some time ago, and I wondered to myself, "where did that thought come from"? Has this ever happened to you? And then just as soon as I thought about finding credible resources to study and research the "thought world", GOD led me to William Walker Atkinson, Thought Vibration or The Law of Attraction in The Thought World. I call this synchronicity and it happens often along this journey.

As I listened to Dr. Atkinson, I could feel his words resonating with me. Not because I admired the author; I had never heard of Dr. Atkinson before now, but the words he spoke caused a reaction in my being. Jesus said this best, "The words I speak unto you are spirit (Vibration/Frequency) and life" (John 6:63, KJV). You can also relate this phenomenon to a piano. If you press and sustain/damper pedal on a piano and sing a note, the string of that same note on the piano, will vibrate when you stop singing. You can hear the piano sounding the same note. When the vibration from one object causes another object to vibrate, it is called resonance.[6] Fascinating, isn't it? Being tuned to the same frequency as your desire, is the focus and has similar effects. This is one of the laws of the universe at work. And this also applies to all of us, being aligned with that which resonates with us.

Words are alive! Search the scripture for yourself. But the Bible is not the only book that attest to this fact. There are other ancient books, scrolls, and other valuable documents that were kept hidden from mainstream society and other public religious venues. Only those who are seriously seeking truth will be led to what is needed for that stage of your journey.

When you progress to the next stage, knowledge will appear to aid and guide you at that stage of your journey. This bears repeating...when you make your commitment to change your life and fulfill your purpose, keep in mind your inner man will only accept information that resonates with you. Another familiar, biblical quote is the Spirit bears witness to the spirit.

For me, I can see so clearly how the Spirit world and the world of vibration/frequency are connected. And now it all makes sense in my head. I was led to study the word "Spirit" and I had an epiphany about my being and existence. Quantum Theory can prove that everything in the Universe and humankind are composed of the same subatomic material (energy), which cannot be created nor destroyed. This is a simplistic way of putting it; nevertheless, the fact remains the same. Most of us do not think of humankind from this viewpoint; but you should because this proves we are ALL connected from a scientific standpoint and down to the cellular level of our being.

Although, this was a huge revelation for me, I am still seeking, because I know there is more to uncover. That's what it means to me

---

[6] https://www.sciencelearn.org.nz/resources/2815-sound-resonance#:~:text=If%20you%20press%20the%20sustain,vibrate%2C%20it%20is%20called%20resonance.

when the Bible states, "Seek and ye shall find; knock and the door shall be opened". Now, there may be some who may say, "That's not what that mean"! My reply to this is, "This isn't what it means to you"! You see, that's what makes this journey so great. It is an individual personal path and no two are alike. Just like fingerprints.

Let's talk more about the Law of Vibration and how this law affects our daily lives. Did you know that everything in existence is constantly in motion? Whether you can see this movement with the naked eye or not; does not negate this fact. Everything is always moving and has a frequency that measure the rate of motion.

Our words and thoughts are no different. Based on one's state of being (feelings and emotions), you choose your life events on purpose or by default. Either way, you are creating your lifestyle ongoing. Choice is a powerful gift freely given to us to use to help us navigate in this physical realm. But to unlock the power contained within "choice" you must meditate on how choices affects your daily life. Choose to live from a space that expresses the highest version of YOURself. This is the soul's purpose and desire. To experience the highest, most joyous, expression of itself in this physical plane.

To connect with the world of creation, you must connect to and communicate with this world using its familiar language and this by way of implementing the Law of Attraction and the Law of Vibration. This world of creation is the plane you begin your work, that is, creating the life you desire. In depth study of the Laws of the Universe is recommended so that you can understand how the laws operate. Once you grasp a basic understanding of this invisible and metaphysical world, you will make the connections and suddenly, so many revelations will come into focus with much clearer understanding.

I became inspired and interested in engraving. I began my research looking into engraving rocks as pet reminders, bringing back an old simple practice. That is, having a pet rock that becomes a focal point for whatever you choose. I could feel my enthusiasm as

I thought about how I could create something special for someone, anyone...because we are all special. I knew it was a matter of time before I embark on a creative and fun adventure. I enjoy working on small projects that bring so much joy during its creation. One day I plan to create mementos to complement this book. You too may become inspired along your journey to start a new hobby or pursue a dream you thought was impossible.

After being enthused to start a new hobby, unbeknownst to me, I became aware of instinct versus intuition. When you first look at both words, they appear to mean the same. But for me, somehow, there is a subtle difference. Instinct is about me having an urge or force driving me to do something without having any knowledge as to why I feel I must perform this thing, or that you can even perform the task (fight or flight). On the other hand, intuition goes further. Intuition is a knowing deep within your being and sometimes, this may be contrary to what others may think. You know what you know based on the inner witness within. This bears repeating, whatever resonates with you, here's a hint...follow your intuition.

For some of us, changing our lives include improving our financial status. Living paycheck to paycheck is not fun and does not cause one to jump for joy. But there is hope that all this can change, and the process starts now. Because money is a high positive frequency, thinking about how the use of money comes into play in your fulfilled desire, creates a GOOD feeling, which is positive. Having this positive feeling aligns with the frequency of money in the Universe and its benefits.

You want to focus on thoughts that are of high positive vibration so that you can create a ripple in the thought world to aid in manifesting your goals. Once you make up your mind about what you choose for your life, do not change your mind. Once your mind is made up, the entire Universe is set in motion to move things around on your behalf. When you change your mind, everything stops.

Remove any negative thoughts that lead to negative feelings that lead to negative emotions that lead to negative energy generating low vibration that connect with all the other negative and low vibrations in the Universe. When you begin your journey and study the Law of Attraction, one of the first major milestone to overcome is the fact that the lifestyle, whatever that is for you, you are now living, is by your design. You put the wheels in motion when you fail to be mindful of your thought life.

Your thoughts run rampant when you are not aware of what you are thinking. Then, you think to yourself or wonder, I did not want this kind of life for myself. Or take the negative vibration approach and yell at me, "this is, you know BS! mumbo jumbo!" But just stay with me and keep an open mind before you dismiss this notion. Some of us, if not most of us have heard the sayings, "You are what you think all day long", "You will have what you say", "The words I speak unto you, they are spirit and they are life". These are just a few well know adages and scriptures that attest to this known fact. Now, what some people do is reframe this scripture to exclude its meaning from creating their current lifestyle. They fail to make the connection, by repeating their current state of lack and proclaiming always being broke. As you can see, the law is working.

I had to come to this sobering conclusion and accept the fact that I am responsible for where I am in my life today. This includes moral character, integrity, wealth, spirituality, generosity, etc..... everything that makes me, ME. Now, the question is how do you feel about the person who stares back at you in the mirror?

When one thinks a thought, ever wonder what happens to that thought which crosses your mind? I heard a well-known spiritual teacher say an individual has approximately 60,000 thoughts per day, each day. We've already established that thoughts are energy that manifest its contents. Now, consider this notion for just a moment because I want you to see the entire picture. Think about all the thought vibration that has existed since the beginning of humankind and all the thoughts that continue to go forth from mankind today. Wow! That's a lot of thinking. So let's make happy thoughts!

While writing this book, there was so much positive vibration flowing, I felt like I'd explode. I continue to focus on good vibration and attune to the frequency and vibration of love and joy. If you are struggling to lift your vibrations to positive vibes, think about a special loved one or special event in your life that brought you joy. This works and is so simple to use.

As you focus on this loved one or special event, happy memories will flood your mind and you <u>will</u> experience your emotions and state of being changing to a state aligned with other positive vibrations. Maintaining a laser focus on my purpose and how this affects humankind, allows me to retain a mindset of the life I desire and ensure positive vibrations continue flowing.

You must become the thing you are seeking. For instance, if you are seeking money, study every belief you have about money to understand its energy and how you relate to that energy. If you resent others with money, you will block the flow of the energy of money. Recognize that money is a tool we use to exchange goods, products, and services.

Since money is vital to our existence, today I focus on taking care of personal business. There are times when you want to concentrate on self-work; but there are other important matters that require your attention as well. So, where does this leave you as far as doing your inner work. Well, there comes a time when you must practice what you preach. It is important to stay on top of business affairs, but always find time at the end of your day to put in some work. Always attempt to do at least one thing that gets you one step closer to achieving your goal.

Sometimes, taking care of business requires your patience during these times. You may not remember this, but at some point, in your life you either thought about being more patient or you knew this is an area that requires inner work and now it's time to practice. It happens to me all the time and it happens to some of you.

Understanding the laws of the universe can be daunting. But don't despair! Again, I had been so skeptical about all this new information I was led to study; and at a lost as to how to process this information and to share with you. But I did process the information and am sharing with you what worked for me in developing a schedule to begin silent sessions in private. Be consistent in spending time in your secret closet as you study new information. God will explain or reveal answers to any questions you have...just ask Him. He is waiting with open arms for you to ask.

Now that you are on your way, it is very important to journal every single day, especially when starting out. Capitalize every moment of the day by practicing being mindful of your "thinking" as you go about your day. If you are facing a crisis or dilemma, it is crucial that you pay close attention to your thoughts and your daily routine conversations. Listen to yourself when you engage in a conversation with someone else. Pay attention to the tone of the conversation and whether its positive or negative. This is a great way to gauge progress.

When I first began this practice, I was astounded as to all the negative words I spoke, and I also paid close attention to the context of my spoken words. What a wake-up call! I'm beginning to understand why I'm discontent with my state of being. I spoke a world of creation into the physical world, and I wasn't even focusing on manifesting. Now, just think about if we set purposeful intent, there is nothing we won't be able to accomplish using our imagination. Can you imagine what you can achieve?

After we become accustomed to the lifestyle we created by default, we may feel stuck and then we settle and give up any hope of ever living the life we covet from a distance. So, instead of deciding to get up and create the life you desire to manifest, you stew in your own pity and sorrow and complain about how bad life is for you and how unfair it is.

Life is not going to change magically by you wishing and hoping life gets better. It does require effort and commitment on your part to put in the necessary time and work to effect the change you desire. In the acknowledgement section, a list of resources is provided as an example of tools and apps I found useful.

The first thing I did was create an atmosphere for writing and meditation. I did not have a lot of space to work with, but I was determined to get started so I improvised and made use of what was available to me. You too, must do whatever you need to do to create a space to do your inner work. This can be a section of a room if no other room is available. Just ensure you can close yourself off from the rest of the house or apartment and enter your secret closet (seeking within) and close the door.

Once you are in your secret closet, you ask yourself, "where do I start?" well, if that's what come to mind, acknowledge your thoughts. This may be the first time you have attempted to get to know yourself, so it will take discipline to learn to be mindful of your thought-life and become aware of what you are thinking. During this time, I ask questions of myself about anything I am in distress about, questions about scripture, whatever comes to mind, I entertain that thought.

The first couple of weeks, I did not see a noticeable change, initially; but before I realized what was happening, I found myself looking forward to entering my secret closet. Because of the repetitive work and setting aside time for meditation and reflection, I was forming a habit of spending quiet time alone in my secret closet. When I recognized a habit was forming, I became aware that this is the first sure-fire sign, that God is responding to my work on my behalf. It felt fantastic! I had measurable result after such a short time of inner work. Isn't that amazing?

The more time I spent alone in my closet, the more I look

forward to alone sessions. Take special note of any experience you have during quiet times and remain vigilant, making note to observe your state of being and mindset. This was a healing process for me too, as I dealt with unresolved issues that surfaced during my quiet times. This cleansing process can be a challenge, especially if you are caught off guard, but it is important to work through these thoughts and feelings. You'd be amazed how liberating this can be.

A lot of times we bury past hurts and unforgiveness that remain unresolved. As a result, we form a protective coating around our sore spots so that nothing can penetrate that area because when anything touches that "sore" spot, we withdrawn. As a warning, let me remind you, whatever that area of your life is that is buried so deep and is being heavily guarded, it's going to continue to resurface until you deal with that situation. This is how you know you are growing... there will be growing pains.

The excitement is building up now, you are starting to gain traction and plowing ahead uphill. Now we all have some idea of what it means to go uphill towing a load of anything. And a lot of us have a lot of BAGGAGE. We must adjust the vehicle used for towing and not only make those adjustments, but other adjustments and variations must be made to successfully climb that hill. This journey is no different and can be compared to towing uphill carrying a load of baggage.

Each of our baggage is very different; but the outcome is the same. You are reading this book because at some point in your life you already made the decision to begin this journey. If you look back over your entire life and retrace your footsteps, amazingly enough, you will find they always lead back to YOURself. Before you disagree, just do it! And be sure to take everything into account before coming to your conclusion.

We are drawn to discover what this life is all about even if we think we are in no position to do anything about it, so we think.

But as you will come to KNOW, we all have a role to play in this physical plane and none are esteemed above the other. This is how life's design works! There's so much more to this than I can explain as this is not the focus of this chapter or book.

CHAPTER THREE

THE VISITOR

We live in a society that is governed by authorities, religions, guidelines, rules, and regulations, all of which are necessary to maintain some form of order in this society. As we embark on this journey, knowingly or unknowingly, the first exposure to a form of authority is being reared under the authority of our parents or other caretakers. This is where the belief system is developed, thus building a mindset based on that set of beliefs and value system.

This is the foundation that is justified by the authority of organized religions, political and military leaders, and other authority figures that play major roles in shaping our worldview. But did you ever wonder how all this (world system), came into existence for the "first" time? A phenomenon of this magnitude requires an in-depth step back from this physical realm and explore this from an "out of mind" perspective. You see, one must get out of his mind-set to understand the "first cause"[7] phenomenon and the realm of the relative.

So, let's talk politics and other organizational structures that govern society. Do you know what politics, religious organizational

---

[7] https://www.newworldencyclopedia.org/entry/First_Cause#:~:text= First%20Cause%20is%20term%20introduced,in%20a%20chain%2C%20 stretching%20backward.

structure, and the organizational structure of the military and perhaps all other business models, have in common? If you study the structure of the Roman Empire, you will find a striking resemblance. This is where politics and religion met and introduced to the known world during the fourth century. Now, I'm no theologian nor am I a historian; but I do have a mind, will, and a determination to understand there is more to humankind's existence, than meets the eye. According to Dr. Elaine Pagels research, a clear and undisputable model designed to maintain control and structure of a growing empire had to be in place to govern the growing masses. Study this for yourself and develop an enlightened knowledge of history, particularly Biblical history.

Did it ever occur to you, there must be more in this life or thought there is something missing? I certainly have! As a small child, I remember wondering to myself where does the wind come from and what's above the clouds. At the time, I had no idea or concept of space or the cosmos. But there has always been a silent knowing within, and now I KNOW it takes time to realize how to unlock what has been locked away. You have the power to create life by design, instead of default; but it does take work regardless of your approach.

As humankind, once you embrace life and dive in with everything you've got, oftentimes, life begins to take shape from the perspective one holds close to one's heart. Now is the perfect time to stop for a minute or two, and examine what's close to your heart, and how does what you hold close to your heart, make you feel. If the worldview you hold close to you evokes a negative reaction, think about what you can do to effect the change you want. This step is always necessary and must be taken by you.

Accepting your current lifestyle being designed by you is an acknowledgment of what your inner world entails. If your life is filled with turmoil, check your inner world and your thought life. Can you focus on a thought long enough to count to ten without losing your concentration? If not, this may be an indication you have lost sight of your soul's desire to experience the highest form of itself in the physical world.

Are you feeling without hope and in a vicious never-ending cycle? Feeling sad and alone? All these thoughts are coming from within your being because there is nothing more to pull from so to speak. When you are no longer feeling positive vibrations, examine your thought-life. This is a sure way to monitor your state of being, moment by moment. You must fill your well so that it does not run dry. Simple fact, but so profound.

Now that we are inhabitants of the earth, we've learned to assimilate in this new environment that is foreign to our being. Just as we are born into the physical realm, we too must be born of the Spirit realm, from whence we came. Once conceived in the spiritual womb, the seed must incubate after conception; and birth is inevitable; This can be compared to the inner work one does in your secret closet. This is also symbolic of the birth process in the physical realm; where we live and where time must elapse before manifestation. For every heavenly metaphor, there is earthly counterpart.

Now, it's time to give birth. As above so below! And so, it is in the spirit world. Some of you may have heard this adage before, but not had an actual experience. Any mother who has given birth to a child can tell you the closer to the delivery date, the more uncomfortable the nurturing stage (pregnancy).

Again, as above so below! Imagine for a moment, your dream, goal, or purpose is fulfilled. This is where your ongoing focus should be. But before you experience your achievements, you must go through the process of nurturing just as a mother nurtures her unborn child. A mother eats the food which nourishes both her physical body as well as the body of her unborn child. And to ensure that both she and the child are in optimal health during the development stage, potent multivitamins are provided for additional nutrients not provided by the regular diet. Your inner work are your multivitamins for optimal experience.

I used this metaphor to illustrate what happens on this journey. Your journey is your pathway to realize your purpose in this life experience and how this realization impacts the overall wellbeing of humankind. It has been said, if you put the needs of others above one's own, your needs will be met automatically. To understand this in proper context, allow me to explain what this meant to me.

When a burning desire is stirred in my inner being, I pay attention to what is being said or better yet, felt. This intense feeling or desire is something that propels me to not forsake my journey. It's easy to say, I'll skip today because I have been so good…. But I did not stop traveling before reaching my destination. Enjoy the road trip and pay attention to the scenery and especially those you encounter along the way. Again, a metaphor for your journey. You will encounter others to help you on your way. This is a good place to remind you to be mindful of what Jesus said about "Lo, I am with you always and I will never leave you or forsake you."

Most of us interpret Jesus' saying "always" as to mean the second half of the above statement, and that is true; but this meant something more to me in addition to his "presence never leaving me". It also means for me and you too, if you choose to believe so, Jesus is with us in ALL WAYS too. Meditate on this for a moment and you will recognize all the ways Jesus, God, and the whole Universe is speaking to all of us individually as well as collectively; continuously, ongoing, nonstop, in all ways; we must pay attention to what is occurring around us. Once I conceptualized this notion, I chose to have an experience of this well-known fact; and so, I did; and I have, and now I AM ONE with I AM.

I am now aware of my being and who I really AM. The next hurdle to jump so to speak, is how do I exist in this place call Earth. Before I attempt to explain how I came to remember who I AM, other factors should be explained to have some kind of place of reference so that you may recognize and realize the point I'm trying to make. This will aid in remembering who you really ARE.

To help you understand how to maneuver on this earthly plane in a physical body, we need to talk about the world and the state of being we all designed by default for ourselves. Believe it or not, your choice, we all had a hand in designing this world system that now governs this world. You may think that you are "just one person, one individual," what did "I" do? Well, I'm glad you asked! Chapter Two and Chapter Four go in depth discussing the roles we play.

Now that you are somewhat enlightened, let's dive into the mechanics of existence in the physical world. As I mentioned earlier, you must step out of your conscious mind and think from a spiritual perspective. Having said that, consider this…we are spiritual beings, living in a body that is encased with what we know to be our soul. All my life I live with the notion that my soul resides in my body. Keep in mind that I'm speaking from my paradigm of existence, and this is my <u>truth</u>.

Knowing that you are first a spiritual being, then a physical being encased with a soul in and around this physical body, is the beginning of understanding who you really are. Our soul is what connects us to God and to each other. Yes, we are all connected and living from this space, is the beginning of knowing who you really are. Being a spiritual being for me means I am an individual expression of God, created in His image. That image cannot be a physical form as we know it, although God may choose to take any form he chooses. But his image is His essence or lifeforce known as Spirit… And yet, I AM created in that image. This may sound mundane to many of you, but I have come to know and experience what this means. I do not know what this may look like to you, but this revelation was the beginning of grasping who I really AM.

Back to being created in God's image. I began to meditate on this which led me to conduct a word study on the word "spirit", which led back to "soul". Interestingly enough, this opened my mind to continue seeking truth for myself. At this stage of my journey, I've just begun and not even scratch the surface of what I remember, found familiar, and experienced on my ongoing journey.

To exist from the spiritual realm in an earthly physical body required me to have a radical shift in mindset. And to do this, I had to find out for myself what this life is all about. It no longer mattered what others have said about this journey, there's no better way to experience life, other than to experience life, for oneself; and that's what I'm doing.... or rather being.

Living in this world as a senior female African American, I managed to survive during the chaos we all created; but I'm no longer satisfied with what we've created and I chose to do something about it and as an individual, it begins with me. For me to see the change I desire for humankind, I must effect change to affect the world. If all of us take responsibility for our contribution to this chaotic world, we all can effect change based on the role we play in this game call life. We all play different roles; some not as glamorous as others; but the roles we all play affect the great Mind of Collective Consciousness. As you continue to read, I go into more detail about Collective Consciousness as it was revealed to me.

So, to sum it all up, yes, I am a spiritual being with a physical body, having an earthly experience on this planet called Earth. I also realize that my entire being, soul and all, and you as well, are surrounded by the soul of God and the Universe. Again, this is how we are One. We don't become One, we are already One, just by mere existence and being HERE NOW. There is a logion in the Gospel of Thomas that explains who we really are, rather perfect...

> "50 Jesus said, "If they say to you, 'Where have you come from?' say to them, 'We have come from the light, from the place where the light came into being by itself, established [itself], and appeared in their image.' If they say to you, 'Is it you?' say, 'We are its

children, and we are the chosen of the living Father.'
If they ask you, 'What is the evidence of your Father
in you?' say to them, 'It is motion and rest.'"[8]

I found this to be my truth and when the dots were connected,
I began to remember things I never knew from an unknown space
of awareness I had never experienced. And this is how I KNOW it
is God speaking because, these revelations are received from a space
greater than myself. This is the reward of my ongoing seeking and
seeking and seeking truth. This is the place that we live from in this
relative plane called Earth to understand why things are the way
they are.

Up to this point of my journey, the above information had not
been revealed but I thought I would share what I know to be true
for those who may need some assurance of knowing that you do
count and matter in ways your mind has not conceived of. I am here
to offer hope to the hopeless, love to the loveless, joy to the joyless,
prosperity to the impoverished because these are the attributes, I
chose for myself as there is virtue in these, so, I chose to think on
these things (Phil 4:8, KJV).

Once you become aware of who you really are, you too, will feel
compelled to share your experiences with those you encounter. A
renewed sense of vitality for life is truly like a living spring flowing
with love throughout your entire being. I have never felt anything
like this!

I titled this chapter "The Visitor" intentionally. Have you ever
heard something that seem so unbelievable? Something straight out
of a Science Fiction movie? This was my first reaction to a truth
that revealed a startling metaphor while conducting research on my
journey.

After realizing who I really AM, it occurred to me this sounds

---

[8] https://www.pbs.org/wgbh/pages/frontline/shows/religion/maps/primary/
gthomas.html

like a Sci-Fi movie. I thought about this more intently… and it hit me all of a sudden… this is exactly what this is! We are in this world; but we are not of this world.[9] Is this otherworldly or what? We are light beings taking shape in the form of this body, encased by our individual soul. Wow…talk about Roswell!

As a parent, it is our responsibility for ensuring the safe transport of other new souls yelling to experience this event called life. And so another conception, another birth, another soul beginning to experience the process of life (conception, birth, and ascension); and you are that soul. Just think about this…. Isn't the entire circle of life amazing? There is so much more to this story than this simplistic version presented here. But you get the idea.

Now that you know that you are an alien, how do you live in an environment that is contrary to your home in the Absolute Realm. This is a good place to attempt to explain the difference between the Spiritual/Absolute Realm and the Physical/Relative Realm.

Before I tell you how I came to KNOW this, I must share with you, even before I knew of such knowledge, I journaled about this concept intuitively. Another perfect example of being divinely guided once you open your heart and allow Jesus to navigate. The joy truly is in the journey!

To understand how to exist and express the highest version of yourself, you must not only know the rules of the game so to speak; but one must know how to facilitate moves when playing the game and have no doubt about who you really are. And most importantly, you must KNOW that the stage for the performance of your life is played out in the physical realm; but you must apply spiritual laws to recognize what's taking place on stage. Once you KNOW and understand how to implement these subtle little tactics, you will come to KNOW and EXPERIENCE LIFE to its fullest, fulfilling

---

[9] https://www.kingjamesbibleonline.org/Bible-Verses-About-Not-Of-This-World/

every dream, goal, aim, purpose… whatever is your soul's desire, can be manifested in your NOW HERE moment.

Back to discussing the physical and spiritual realms. Chapter One briefly touched on the subject of Quantum Theory, and I have come to understand how this area of science offers very definitive data regarding this "stuff" that is found throughout and in everything in the Universe. Scientists and Physicists have observed this microscopic universe at the quark[10] level, and groundbreaking information is on the brink of revolutionizing medicine and how we view the universe based on information in the NOW… because tomorrow it may look different, as these overlapping energies are always in motion.

But what makes this so amazing, we are a living form of intelligent energy with an intellect that has the ability to EXPERIENCE LIFE in the physical world in a physical body. This is the gift of life God chose to freely give to us. Problem with this kind of thinking, it goes against everything you may believe or ever been taught. But I found this knowledge useful in helping me understand the essence of my being at the highest level. Can you see this from a scientific and spiritual perspective? I do!

This is how it was revealed to me. God created us in His image. That image can only be Light, since God takes on no physical form, unless He chooses to do so. But that Light consists of energy, intelligence, wisdom, creative power, and PURE LOVE. God is ALL these things and the thing He is NOT. Where can you turn and not find God's Presence? But just because God is ALL in ALL and through ALL, does not mean God is going to interfere in the affairs of man. God has said over and over again, I give you keys to the Kingdom all you have to do is spend time with me and what is hidden there for you will be revealed. But until man unify as a force of One to effect change for the mutual benefit of ALL, we

---

10   https://en.wikipedia.org/wiki/Quark

will continue on this same destructive path of living apart from recognizing that we are ALL connected and must become unified as One working in unison for the mutual benefit of ALL.

Coming together as One is no small feat; although, not impossible. It all starts with each of us individually. When we recognize who we really are and the power we possess, we can literally move mountains. Dedicate fifteen minutes of your time each day to appreciate LIFE in ALL things and open your heart to allow Jesus to come in and reveal Himself to you.

We have become so segregated in our thinking and ability to work together, we would rather see the destruction of the world as we know it today, than to come together to implement a solution. Talk about self-destructive behavior and thinking. This is not the space one should live from day in and day out.

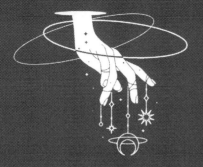

PART II

INSIDE THE MATRIX

CHAPTER FOUR

THE MAN IN CHARGE (EGO)

It's time to talk about the elephant in the room, the Ego. Some of you may have some knowledge about what the ego is and how it affects our day-to-day experiences. People love being at the top of their game, regardless of what it is. And it usually comes at the expense of others.

I noticed today I was aware of my emotional state shifting to an unpleasant mood when I became late for an appointment. I'm grateful I became immediately aware of how my feelings changed… just for a moment. I brought myself to my NOW HERE moment, aware that this is an opportunity to force myself to not have an old familiar reaction and "go there". It was a struggle to fight against my ego to shift from wanting to throw a fit to changing my thoughts to something more pleasant. The "ego" wants to have its way regardless of the harm it may cause.

It took effort, but I finally did change my state of being to something more pleasant. Key is being mindful when you have a change in your feelings that causes a shift in your state of being. Ask yourself what caused this to happen and if you can't do anything to change the situation, think about something more pleasant. I know you may not want to, but believe me, it's worth it in the end because thoughts are things, and you must be careful about what thoughts you're thinking. You just may create something you don't want. The small subtle changes create the greatest impact.

I'm constantly hearing ideas and thoughts running through my mind as this work of art (this book) takes form. I am so thankful and grateful that God is literally speaking to me in phrases, which leads to insights and information to share. This is so amazing! And this is how I know that GOD is writing this book instead of me writing from my egoic perspective.

I am by no means an expert on the "ego", I leave that up to Freud, who is well-known and respected in the scholarly world of Psychology and Psychiatry. As I stated above, I am no expert; however, I did earn a bachelor's degree in Psychology so I may speak as a learned student on the subject just for a moment. My summation of the ego is just that! My summation.

Understanding the ego and how it affects your life requires you to be aware of the subtle little things that disturb you within. If there is any kind of reaction that creates an uneasy feeling, you should pay attention, because something is seeking your attention. Examine yourself in depth to uncover whatever is hidden. You will be astonished as to how quickly self-examination will become automatic because you have trained yourself to be aware of your inner world.

It's the little steps that are made consistently that create monumental change effortless. Do not take my word as final; however, I encourage everyone to do their due diligence. Part IV of this book provides more insight into the rewards of due diligence. Study for yourself, allowing Jesus to uncover what is hidden inside of you. Again, this book is meant to be an easy and practical read.

Some of you may have wondered about your reason for existence during this lifetime. No matter your reason, I know this book can provide some help you may have been searching for your entire life. Whether we are aware of it or not, deep down we all are trying to return to whence we came and that is to our Creator. We are like a sliver of God's essence and may be compared to a wave in the ocean.

Inside this Matrix (physical realm) is an invisible set of intricate systems that have evolved into a stream of governments, worldly management systems, technological moguls, political and social constructs, and all the woes we created by faulty designs and unconscious thoughts.

I ponder this…if thoughts create things, then all the thoughts from the beginning of humankind have created the Mind of Consciousness that exists simultaneously alongside the physical world…. that is, the Relative Realm. Now this seems straightforward on the surface; but take it from me, there is so much more to study. More on this later, which leads me to "roles". Everybody has one, whether you know it or not. And even that may be your role.

Understanding roles will alleviate a lot of your frustrations. If one is an ass, just remember s/he is playing his/her role well. Just an observation regarding roles! You can use this simple trick to view life from a new perspective and at the same time increase your GOOD vibration. Either way, you have a win/win mindset.

Maintaining a positive mindset is always the goal. This is perfect for when you are driving and get cut off. Instead of allowing someone else to cause you to deplete your energy and upset your NOW moment, remember it's just a role being played out until that individual evolves into a higher level of beingness.

This simple technique can be used for nearly every situation. Just think, regardless of the individual, just view individuals' actions as a role they are playing and are a means to an end; remember we are connected and what I do affect others and what others do affect me. This simple switch in mindset has helped me keep my ego in check as well as maintain GOOD vibration.

The Bible also speaks on the roles we play in this physical realm. I Cor. 12, is a great place to understand the roles and administrations that are in place to ensure we have everything we need to fulfill our purpose in expressing who we really are. And when those roles appear contrary to what we knew to be true based on past scriptural teachings; we are to curse not the things that appear to bring calamity, but to bless it because this is an indication you are on the right track to remembering who you really are. This is a key to understanding how to maneuver in the Relative Realm.

I know this sounds contradictory; but if you think about it, we do this when something unpleasant occurs and depletes our positive vibration. We tend to get into a "funk" and live there far too long. Again, curse not the thing that bring calamities or unpleasant experiences; but bless that thing and use that as an opportunity to grow and check the EGO. This is how you let your light shine in the darkness. Come to your senses! Get up and come back home.

To come home is to go within and search yourself and ask yourself questions and seek answers to those questions. Remember, this journey is about you and your remembrance of who you really are and our purpose for existing on this physical plane. When you begin to ask yourself questions, you will find that the answers show up one way or another. This happens to me each time I come across a concept I am unfamiliar with, I go within to seek answers to my questions and 10/10 times, the answer is revealed to me. Life is so wonderful. Keep in mind, the *ego* is your greatest stumbling block for growth.

Now let's talk about the ego-driven individual that is so self-assured and confident, s/he has discovered a hidden truth. On the surface, there is nothing wrong with living from a "grandiose" personality; but it must be kept in check. Case in point; when you begin to remember elements of the spiritual realm, if one is not careful, accessing this knowledge can lead to inappropriate application of this newfound knowledge; thereby, living from a space of arrogance and haughtiness that hinders the progress of humankind. This is not the state of being the soul is seeking to EXPERIENCE. It seeks to experience the highest and the best version of itself.

God has provided us with all the attributes we need to experience a life filled with the joy and love we all so desire to experience; a life free of concern and worry; a utopia if I may ... a Garden of Eden where, no serpent is waiting to deceive us by perpetrating one of the greatest deception of them all.

This is one of many dogmas we have accepted as truth; and this truth states that if we fail to live up to God's standards (Gods' word stated according to what man wrote), we are doomed and will spend an eternity in torment and torture.

Organized religion too, has a matrix, so to speak, inside the Relative Realm. Eighty-five percent or more of humanity believe in an Entity referred to as God, Allah, Jehovah, the Universe, the Source...a higher power that exist outside of one's being that is responsible for our existence.

Regardless of what this power or Infinite Intelligence is called, its existence IS ALL THERE IS. It is the Great Unseen. It was there before in the beginning of beginnings. Now that most of us can agree on this fact, we can fast-forward to how ALL THAT IS chose to create a world for His creation of beings that He created for His good pleasure and enjoyment. The Apostle Paul wrote in Philippians 2:13-18 ...

> **13**For it is God which worketh in you both to will and to do of *his* good pleasure. **14**Do all things without murmurings and disputings: **15**That ye may be blameless and harmless, the sons of God, without rebuke, in the midst of a crooked and perverse nation, among whom ye shine as lights in the world; **16**Holding forth the word of life; that I may rejoice in the day of Christ, that I have not run in vain, neither laboured in vain. **17**Yea, and if I be offered upon the sacrifice and service of your faith,

I joy, and rejoice with you all. **18**For the same cause
also do ye joy and rejoice with me.[11]

So, what does this mean, God creating us for *his* good pleasure?
I insist on repeating that this is <u>my journey</u> and <u>my truth</u>. You
must embark on your journey for yourself and seek your truth to
remember who you really are. God revealed to me that He is ALL
THAT THERE IS and is in a perfect state of being, existing in the
Absolute Realm in all its glory and magnificence. There is nothing
else that exists in the realm of where God resides, except the Spirit
of God that is PURE LOVE. A LOVE so PURE that it wants,
needs, or demands nothing from us in return for His unconditional
PURE LOVE.

On the other hand, organized religions paint an entirely different
picture that God is jealous, judgmental, condemning, vengeful, and
angry; and will punish those who do not make a particular confession,
say a certain prayer, buy your soul out of purgatory, face the East to
pray three times a day, and on and on it goes. God requires none of
these things from us. And if He did, what would be the purpose?
Again, God neither wants nothing, needs nothing, or requires
nothing from us in return for his PURE, UNCONDITIONAL,
BLISSFUL LOVE. Can you see the contradiction here?

So, for us to bring God joy and pleasure, He had to devise a
plan for Himself to experience pleasure in all its many wonderful
and magnificent ways. This is where we, as humankind, comes in.
Depending on the region one may live, determines who was sent to
mankind to remind us of who we really are.

Jesus, Mohammad, Buddha, Patanjali, the Dali Lama, and
on and on we can list those who have walked before us, as the
embodiment of this truth. I ascribe to the deity Jesus, the Christ,
who demonstrated how to live in this physical realm, as a spiritual
entity residing in a body encased with a soul and walking with the

---

[11] https://biblehub.com/kjv/philippians/2.htm

authority of the Father. Jesus made it known; his mission is to fulfill that of our Father. By fulfilling His divine purpose, God recognized Jesus' accomplishment as "man" and said he was "well pleased".

I recognized that Jesus is the embodiment of the likeness of God living in a body in the physical plane and that he conquered all the adversities that challenged his "beingness." Jesus and others who taught and spoke of this intelligent and infinite power within, made it simplistically clear, we have this same power flowing in us, and we too, can overcome adversities and rise to the occasion; but we must go within to remember who we really are, if we are to understand how life works in the physical plane.

As you progress through this book and subsequent chapters, be open minded and allow your inner man to guide you once you recognize the signposts along your path. And you will recognize the signs and will be reminded within when this happens. You don't have to strive for this to happen; it just does! This is one of the things that makes this journey so wonderful.

When you begin to experience life and scripture and not just from a space KNOWING, but from a space of EXPERIENCE, life truly does come ALIVE. It is difficult to describe the feeling you experience when you reach this stage of your journey. It's like I heard someone say, "my cup runneth over". And this feeling can be compared to when you are in love with your sweetheart…. it just flows and flows…nothing but PURE BLISSFUL LOVE. I have never felt anything like this or knew that any human can experience such pure love, truth, and joy to this extent and not be carried away. I am so serious!

This is what this journey is all about to start with. There is so much more in store for those who love Him and if this is just the tip of the iceberg, I cannot begin to imagine what else I would want to experience; but I *KNOW* more is coming for me to *EXPERIENCE* so if you want to know the progress…look for sequels as God has already said there will be more to follow.

After realizing I am treading in an area of spirituality that many may find offensive. Let me apologize ahead of time. It is not my intention to offend anyone's religion; but according to another famous author, there are over approximately 4,200 known religions and what I find so astonishing is the fact that none agree on the correct version of God; and to top it off, each religion ascribes their God is the true God. So, how do you determine which God is the true and real God? No wonder there is so much confusion surrounding religion.

God is in every aspect of who I AM. This includes the good, the bad; the rich, the poor; the up, the down of it…the right, the wrong of it; EVERYTHING. And when I embrace the simple fact that God is every aspect of myself, I no longer separate myself or parts of myself from me. God is the same way, he will never alienate parts of Himself (humanity) from Himself, and this is what He is trying to tell us when He said we are ONE.

The parts of ourselves that we do not like, once we recognize those attributes, we choose to change for the better; but we don't isolate that aspect of ourself because we have a bad temper, or are unkind, or wear other unattractive labels. Just as we do not condemn that aspect of self to eternal damnation, neither does God condemn those parts of Himself to eternal damnation.

We must become conscious that we have a choice to choose which aspect of God we choose to experience. Do we want to experience love, or do we want to experience fear; do we want to experience peace, or do we want to experience war… this explains how one man can commit all kind of evil and still return to where he came from. God does not alienate that aspect of Himself, any more than the ocean can alienate itself from the waves as it would no longer be the ocean without its waves.

CHAPTER FIVE

WHERE DID I GO WRONG

I worked hard all my life to provide a good life for my family and it appears that the more I work, the more I need to keep working. No matter how hard I try, life remains a daily struggle. I went to church every Sunday before the pandemic; Now, I either attend virtually or view the streaming services online.

And to make sure I don't be "cursed with a curse", I pay my tithes, follow what my pastor teaches from the Bible, I don't act like a heathen, as do other unruly beings.... You may think to yourself, "I am so glad I'm not like them". The Bible teaches if your righteousness does not exceed the Pharisees, it'll be easier for a camel to go through the eye of a needle, than for the Pharisees to enter the Kingdom of God. Simply put your works and all your "doings" is not the path to the Kingdom of God.

I was so desperate to find answers to my dilemmas and questions about the Bible, I failed to realize the connection between spiritual prosperity and worldly prosperity. I was so caught up with committing to a system I believe would ultimately lead to financial success, I momentarily lost sight of my true purpose.

Life is not so much about destiny because you will reach your fate whether you are sleep-living or aware of your beingness. The outcome is determined based on the choices made up to this point.

Many will dispute this well-known fact; however, you can read your Bible and see for yourself. If you are not familiar with the Bible verses, just think of how you manifested something from just a thought. Whether it was getting that job, that special new car, cute pair of expensive shoes...whatever, bottom line is that you got it. The principle is the same. But when it comes to manifesting wealth, health and other states that seem out of reach, we tend to get stuck and resort back to old behaviors.

When it comes to something we really want and it's a big-ticket item, one tends to think it's out of reach. But again, the principle is the same and works for small goals and accomplishments as well as goals that seem impossible or out of our reach. Just like you manifested those things you consider small or within reach, you can manifest the life you desire. But remember it does take time in the physical plane for goals and desires to manifest.

Key point to remember is to become so familiar with how the laws of the universe operate and compare these laws to your thought life. Take mental note of what you are thinking in the NOW (at this very moment). If it's a negative thought, ask yourself "where did that thought come from?" acknowledge that thought; and if it's an area of your life that requires some work, then look within and get busy. This may be a block to your ability to maintain good vibration; thereby, emitting negative energy and feeling as though GOD has forsaken you.

When this happens, you lose momentum and will need to build that momentum up again and this time, keep it going. Failing to maintain momentum, delays manifestation. Remember, God never leaves us! How can He when he is within and through every one of us no matter who you are, what you may have done, or where you are in life...none of these things matter. Your life can change, and it can start NOW. It's all up to you, no one else is responsible for you, except you.

Working hard in the physical plane is not the only way to

achieve what one may call success. Success is a relative term, and its interpretation is very subjective. To measure one's success, you need to understand what means are used to measure success. We share different ideas of success; therefore, be open to what success looks like for you.

I consider myself to be a success at whatever I set my mind to achieve; however, for me, this required a lot of physical and mental effort to withstand today's work environment and biased ethics. Policies and procedures cause one to doubt who they are because one is treated as though one is just a number and nothing more. When I worked in Corporate America, I added additional stress, wear, and tear to this body so that I may exist in this physical plane in peace. So I thought! And now in my winter years, I have a deeper understanding of LIFE and the importance of the choices I make in my NOW moment. NOW, I find myself just beginning my journey to remember who I really AM.

Initially, I was somewhat at odds about the fact that I am just NOW beginning my journey; but I told myself it is better to start NOW, than to never start at all; and age is insignificant when it comes to this journey. I am so thankful I chose to pursue my truth and it is being revealed to me for such a time as this. I came to realize that everything happens, as it should and there are no mistakes or coincidences.

This would be a good place to revisit past events in your life to put the pieces of the puzzle together. Having an ear to hear and eyes to see is not just to maneuver in the physical realm. One must possess these faculties to interpret the spiritual realm and live from this space as you embark on life events.

We exert so much energy in becoming the best of the best until we lose sight of what really matters. We have forgotten the fundamental intent for our existence…. And believe it or not, it is not the intention of our Creator for man to live in distress by no stretch of the imagination. His intent for us is to experience life in its entirety. Life is meant to be sheer bliss and enjoyment for us in our bodily form and for God Himself. God wants us to experience what He chose to experience, what He knows conceptually, and this is to experience and express His Magnificence in human form, through mankind, that is us.

God desired to experience Himself outside of His perfect dwelling place; and the only way for God to have this experience is for us to have this experience. When we experience joy, love, prosperity, peace, and happiness, God rejoices for His children, because He knows what this feels like and rejoices with us.

All God expects us to do is imitate those who walked before us (Masters of Old) who demonstrated how to live in this earthly physical plane as a spiritual being. This requires nothing on your part, but to seek out to experience the highest and best version of who you really are. Gods requires nothing from us, to enjoy this LIFE EXPERIENCE.

For some strange reason, people don't like hearing God and all this other spooky stuff in the same sentence. Why is this? Again, GOD is ALL there IS, so what is so mysterious about this living and moving energy that is intelligent and is PURE LOVE. Wow…what a rush! We have front row seats to one of the greatest shows in the house to observe the creation of our lives unfold before our very eyes.

CHAPTER SIX

SOMETHING'S GOT TO GIVE

I cannot continue the path that I'm heading. It's a vicious cycle. Every day is the same thing repeatedly. This is the silent mantra of most individuals, and the majority are unaware of this inner mantra. You can count on keeping your current lifestyle regardless of what your lifestyle looks like if you do not implement change. Maintaining this state of being is living your past repeatedly, and yet you wonder why you are not living life from the best version of YOURself. It is now time to get busy.

It's time to wake up and stop SLEEP-LIVING. Sleep-living is living from a state of being where every day is a repeat of the day before. If you looked this word up in the dictionary, you would not find it. This is a new word that just came to me as I'm writing. I made it up! To me, it's only logical (Spock).

Allow me to explain. It is impossible to live life from a laser focus on your intent, and not be impacted by that intent...whatever your intent may be. I can speak candid about this because I can see and feel the power of the Light of Jesus radiating from the depths of my inner being, validating I am a child of the Living Father. I EXPERIENCED this KNOWING, and you can too, once you become aware of who you really are. This is your divine right and purpose.

As I think about how this book may impact billions of people, it is important to maintain a healthy and positive mindset while being in a space of time that may uproot several aspects of my life and others as well. Therefore, I continue to seek truth on its highest level of consciousness. It seems the more I learn, the more I realize what I do not know. This journey is ongoing and ever exciting.

The revelation of this enormous power and the force behind this power is unmistakably divine. For me to gain a deeper revelation of this immense power, I had to gain understanding as well as wisdom to implement the knowledge I was led to comprehend. Wow, what a task, sorting through so much information in the midst of a tormented and divided understanding of how all this information fit perfectly to paint a picture, I so desperately needed to see.

So, when I sat down to write today, it came to me to write about understanding how to use the authority of GOD. All things are possible to him who believes. God revealed to me that He has given us the authority to use His Power on our behalf, because it is our God-given right to do so. But how do we do that?

Upon asking God, how to do that…. that is walk in the authority just as Jesus did when he walked this earth, the next thing I heard was simple logic. What God said to me was not deep theology, but that we are to imitate Jesus in all that he said, mimic his behavior, and KNOW who your Father is, the Source for ALL things. This must become the foundation of your relationship with God in this physical plane. Having this KNOWING leads to EXPERIENCING God's power in ways you cannot begin to imagine. It must become your BEINGNESS on a daily basis. You get what you put into any endeavor; and this EXPERIENCE is no different.

In every instance where Jesus performed miracles for the masses, he lifted his head and gave thanks. Just this one action of giving thanks to the Source of ALL things, is a sure-fire way of communing with GOD and witnessing his power being manifested. As I meditated on this known fact, even I could feel GOD's power and could hear

God's voice speaking to me in a soft and practical manner. I KNOW it's God's voice because of the immense overwhelming loss of control of giving thanks and acknowledging what was spoken and felt, at the same time.

The presence of God may become so intense at times and can cause physical bodily reactions that cannot be disputed. Then I heard within how to use GOD's power. We are to act as GOD (operant power) in this case speak to manifest our creation just as Our Father who are in heaven, did. Remember, we are created in His image and are capable of speaking our creation into the physical plane too. To aid in the manifesting, one can assume the end result, and follow the Golden Rule to ensure mutual benefit for ALL. It is God's good pleasure to give us the kingdom (desires of our heart). Read it for yourself...

God longed to EXPERIENCE Himself through us by enjoying pleasure and other LIFE events in this relative realm. It is impossible to experience anything outside of what exists in the Absolute Realm; therefore, LIFE has to exist in the physical realm to EXPERIENCE the AM-NESS and the AM NOT-NESS of God's divinity so that we can begin to remember who we really are.

Now, to use your innate power of GOD, begin by visualizing a scene of your desire fulfilled, then fix the scene in your mind and assume the feeling of the desire fulfilled, knowing that it's already done and giving thanks to God for hearing and fulfilling your desire. Now put both together (desire fulfilled and giving thanks) when you meditate. You know your Father's name, who is I AM. When you say I AM, this invokes Father and Jesus the Christ within you to move on your behalf.

When I believe and have faith in this authority, I can speak to the mountains, and they step aside. Another important key to remember, you must believe it's ok to act as God in that you are the operant power. I know, sounds like blasphemy but this is what I heard within. It's time to understand the power behind our creation for such a time as this.

The scriptures go on to say, test it to see if it is true. This is another promise from God telling us we can rely on Him being faithful, as he is the *Supreme Being* and we are just *Human Beings.*

> 31But seek His kingdom, and these things will be added unto you. 32Do not be afraid, little flock, for your Father is pleased to give you the kingdom.[12]

You must act as a BEING with a KNOWING that the outcome has already been produced for you and this is what you choose for yourself. Give thanks to God for having heard you and answered you. Let this mindset be in you that was also the mindset of Jesus, the Christ. Believe it will come to pass when you pray (meditate, become your desires…all of them). I searched scripture and it is stated best according to Luke…He walked with the authority of God the Father, and the religious leaders of that time were not familiar with this power and authority Jesus so elegantly demonstrated. And so it is today, most of the religious leaders today will undoubtedly say this is blasphemous rhetoric; but I need no validation from no man, as GOD has already validated me just by my mere existence in this physical plane. And this goes for you. You too, are also validated by GOD and need no man's permission to KNOW and EXPERIENCE the truth for yourself.

I begin to ponder why would the church use religion to control its members and congregation. I'm not throwing any stones, but merely pointing out what I experienced firsthand, during my journey, and these are my observations; I found no consistent spiritual teaching being taught as one having authority as Jesus did.

You hear every kind of themed story, but few have taught how to use the power of God within us. Jesus KNEW He and the Father are One and whatever he desired; it was already done. This is the power and authority Jesus demonstrated in the flesh.

[12] https://biblehub.com/luke/12-31-32.htm

PART III

OUTSIDE THE MATRIX

CHAPTER SEVEN

WHERE DO I BEGIN

Who can I trust to help me find my way without misinformation and/or condemnation? The first step to your journey is to always begin by looking within. Before any change can take place, you must first examine your heart to address any unresolved conflicts with family, friends, coworkers, or any others that cause a negative stir in your heart when you think of that person or incident. Whatever that thing maybe, it must be dealt with; otherwise, this issue will continue to stifle your progress. If a person remains in this state for a prolong period, s/he may give up and succumb to defeat before ever getting started.

We must face ourselves for growth to be measured. Otherwise, how could self-examination yield the desired outcome. I was talking to a friend of mine one day and he said something very profound to me. He said, "You can't miss what you can't measure". I wasn't sure what he meant at the time; however this phrase resonated with me, and I asked if I may use this phrase in this book.

At the time, I was unsure as to how I would be able to use this phrase; but, as you can see, it all worked together for the mutual good of ALL. You see, to measure growth, there must be a standard in place to compare. For example, when you have unforgiveness in your heart towards an individual, when you enter your secret closet, all is revealed, and nothing is hidden from your inner man. Acknowledging this unforgiveness is the beginning of inner work to become the best person you can be. When you face a similar situation, you will immediately be reminded of the previous situation where you were mindful of a state of being generating negative vibration.

When I first began my journey, I did not understand this newfound information and it scared me to the point I was hesitant about pursuing this topic any further. Because of my "Christian" upbringing as a child and adult, I dare not think outside of what I was taught my entire life. I was really terrified! So, I had to meditate for guidance as to how to utilize this information in a way that would be congruent with all I had come to KNOW and UNDERSTAND. Processing this new paradigm shift did not occur overnight. And information continues to be processed daily.

I'd been contemplating which direction to aim this manuscript; but then, I heard from within to write and allow the book to take its own form. Wow!!! I don't know about you, but to me, that is incredible. Where did this thought come from? The scripture is clear about this when it says there is nothing new under the sun. Some may say it applies to this or that; but I believe it applies to just what it says, "nothing new" and to me, that means, everything fits in that description of nothing new.

Once I wrapped my mind around this one scriptural phrase, I became aware of the literal meaning, which, opened a whole new perspective (world) for me. Think about this for just a moment. Imagine for an instant "nothing new under the sun" and be carried away by this simple phrase. Where does your imagination take you?

While reading, some of us tend to just call out words without recognizing the power that is packed in the seed of the words. The Parable of the Sower explains the seed (word) and its magnificent power. This too, takes practice, living in the NOW and feel the vibration behind the power in the word. You must be opened to feel and know with your heart. This too takes practice.

Jesus spoke in the New Testament, that the words I speak are spirit and life. Wow! This scripture is packed with the power to change things. Now take this scripture coupled with the fact that words also have vibration…same thing. The spirit and vibration work the same way. The ability to manifest a new life if you are not living your life to your satisfaction, is achievable. Change is possible, but you will need to commit to the process.

You will have help along the way. So, know that you are not alone. What I do impacts all of us and this goes for you as well. We are all connected. Don't take my word for it! Read Romans 12:5 for yourself. Meditate on this as you lay upon your bed. Feel the impact of the energy released when you conceptualize the fact that we are all connected.

Take notice, God always provide what you need when you are determined to stretch beyond your comfort zone. Remember persistence equals momentum, and momentum equals exponential acceleration. Once you see noticeable changes, you will be motivated to continue seeking and searching for truths that resonates with your highest expression of who you really are.

Our collective actions have a significant impact on our world, good, bad, or indifferent. It does not matter! The Mind of Consciousness created by humankind apparently evolved into our present world with all its elements and states of being. Dr. William Walker Watkinson is a subject matter expert in this area regarding thoughts, vibration, and humankind. I believe that this is where Science and Religion meet once again in the laboratory. This may sound somewhat blasphemous to many, but if GOD is a Spirit, how do you classify his essence?

As I continued my research, I felt a shift of energy from mid to extremely high vibration and I am so grateful. God continues to speak to me about my journey. As I was thinking, it occurred to me when visualizing the result of your chief aim or goal, don't just see yourself as having achieved your goal, but take it a step further and see the result of how your achievement affects the good of humankind. In other words, what will you do for humankind once you find purpose or fulfill your chief aim?

Now that you have everything you've ever wanted in your entire life, what's next? You should have this in mind at the beginning of your journey because this is an aspect of God's personality. God knew the ending from the beginning and regardless of what some people may say, we are creators just as is God. If you don't believe me, look at your world and reflect on your thought-life and the state of your being. Take special note as you look back and pay attention to emotions of love, joy, anger, fear, hate…and examine your state of being during these times.

On your journey, there will be times when you will experience shifts in vibrations (emotions/feelings). It is very important to pay attention to your emotions/feelings because this works like an internal hot/cold meter…hot being equivalent to feeling GOOD. Monitor your meter the moment you become aware of how you are feeling.

Emotions are expressed when there is a change in how you feel. We are influenced by our surroundings and the world we engage daily. How we react to our world is a direct result of the worldview we hold and the information that is constantly being fed into that worldview.

This is why we continue to get what we keep getting in life. Our world of consciousness expands regardless of the kind of information (good/bad, positive/negative) that resonates with us. Now this is a big pill to swallow. Some of you may disagree with this summation; nevertheless, the fact remains valid. Once you develop a particular way of thinking, this mentality is the worldview you hold and everything you encounter is filtered by this worldview. This includes all the opinions, tenets, and other information perceived in your being.

Remember this one thing if you don't remember anything else, use your emotions as a guide to know when you are flowing in well-being. If you feel GOOD, you are flowing in positive vibration, if you are feeling bad, you are flowing in negative vibration. Being mindful of this one simple fact will prove invaluable.

CHAPTER EIGHT

THAT'S NOT WHAT I WAS TAUGHT

On this journey you may encounter ideas and belief systems that will rock the foundation you thought you were planted on. Living from your worldview can be limiting or it can propel you to begin your search for inner peace and the kingdom within.

I was pondering on how to start this manuscript and so many ideas emerged. My intent was to write a practical book that does not require much effort to grasp its content. This book is not intended to be the only guide to fulfilling your desire. It is a testament to the nuggets of truths revealed along this journey. As I opened my heart to my Father God, after becoming disheartened, only then is when I began to find answers to questions that plagued me most of my adult life. Matthew 6:33 is the scripture that drove me to begin my search to realize who I really AM.

It occurred to me before any noticeable changes occur, you must first, above and beyond anything else deal with your inner struggles. We either are going through something or have gone through something; otherwise, you would not be reading this book. In fact, it's very difficult, when you face yourself looking inward, to confront your inner torments and turmoil (Hell) that have not been properly dealt with within.

When you face inward, you will begin to listen to your thoughts and acknowledge what you are thinking. And when you become aware of your thoughts that create negative emotions or feelings, take notice and search within to determine the root cause. This is very important as it will help prevent high and low mood swings. You want to be in high vibration as often as you can to maintain momentum. You should always strive to be the best version of "YOU" that you can be. And this my friend, is no small feat.

Upon recognition of the first signs of remembering something so familiar, I was led to the Gospel of Thomas. I will expound in greater detail, the story behind this gospel and its impact during my quest for truth. Meanwhile, my seeking for wisdom and truth, continues.

Reading and learning about some of the laws of the universe and its connection to God was mind-boggling enough; but then to learn and experience God in a way that has NEVER been taught in any traditional church I've ever attended; was unlike anything I've ever EXPERIENCED.

I am familiar with the teachings of many denominations and the internal operations of members and their leaders. That's enough for me to run in the other direction and seek truth for myself. I tried listening to other leaders and their scriptural teachings, and it worked for a season; but there was still something incomplete about the messages taught and I KNEW in my spirit, there was so much more to God and His Infinite truths.

But this gospel, Gospel of Thomas, was different in its presentation and message. As I studied the Gospel of Thomas according to the work done in the painstaking intense scrutiny and scholarly publication work of Dr. Elaine Pagels, Princeton University, I have a basic knowledge of the incredible power contained in this particular scroll. This scroll is the catalyst that led to my ultimate EXPERIENCE with PURE LOVE, that is GOD.

Not only did I have this amazing EXERIENCE, but I also received so much insight regarding my purpose HERE and NOW.

Additionally, I realize once I KNEW my truth, I must live by this truth, as I am doing so and will continue to do so. This is the most profound epiphany I have ever experienced up to now. And it is so liberating because you can no longer live the life you once lived. Change is occurring right now, and it is inevitable from this point forward as long as you remain faithful to your journey. And it keeps getting better and better.

As I write this, I'm reminded early on my journey, I would always affirm this, "every day in every way, I am getting better and better." Amazing to see how this affirmation manifested in my life experience. People, this is what happens when you put the work in. You can make things happen, but it must happen within you first. Key point: Be the change you wish to see. Then share this with someone else. This is the power of the Universe at work when we connect in this manner. Each one reaching one and sharing with those we encounter, the amazing news of who we really are and our divine purpose in this physical plane.

You will not hear this kind of talk across the majority of pulpits or other podiums religious leaders are using to continue to keep the masses sleep-living. Many religions today for the most part, are used as a mechanism to maintain control over the masses of individuals. Because when one engages in thinking for oneself, you can no longer control or influence others to adapt to the tenets or dogma being promulgated throughout the masses.

If you asked pastors and religious leaders to tell their congregation to stop tithing or giving to the church, for example, what do you think will happen? When one is committed to the work of the ministry, there is no need to demand one to give or perform any tasks; it comes naturally. Stand back and watch what happens if the leaders are brave enough to walk in faith. Not many are willing to take this risk. So, they use the Bible as a weapon of fear to force people to give their last to God. Guess what y'all…. God told me to tell yall he can't spend the money, but the people who takes it can.

So, give because you desire to give and be certain that your giving is done cheerfully and used for the mutual benefit of ALL.

It is far past the time for us to stop allowing others to tell us our truth. They say truth is absolute; and yes, that is true, but not in this earthly plane. You have to understand a lot more about how this universe works and how this world has come to be what it is today.... A conglomerate of bias systems enslaving the minds of the masses. An example of such a system is organized religious and other institutions that enslave the minds of its members by following ritualistic practices to prevent one from thinking for oneself. And all of this nonsense is done in the name of God. The same God of Love, Peace, Joy and so forth and so on. And by the same token, this same God is a God of Judgment, Jealousy, Vengeance and will cast you in the lake of fire for all eternity, if you fall short.

This is the truth I lived by for decades. Of all the versions of truths out there and since everyone's truth is "the truth", according to their teachings, how does one decide which truth to follow? This is the prevailing question that continues to plague humanity.

CHAPTER NINE

I NEED HELP

I have listened to pastors, teachers, and other spiritual leaders in the hopes of hearing something that could help me move from my current state of being. Because of my Christian teaching, it was difficult to see the role I played in creating the life I was NOW living. It wasn't until I begin to search for truth, I finally accepted the fact that I created this life, and it is I who must do something about it. Once I accepted this realization, I had just made the first huge step of impacting the rest of this wonderful life. Stop searching for answers outside of yourself, now that you recognize change is needed and you have made that commitment to begin the process, NOW.

According to the Book of James, to paraphrase the passage, don't just be a hearer of the Word only, but it's long time to be a doer of the Word. It's time to act NOW. At first, it may seem as though nothing is happening within, and this is normal. Remember, you must develop an entire new way of thinking, and this is no small deed; however, it is very achievable. Study Romans 12:1-2 and get a biblical perspective of this new mindset. And if you need another reference, look at 1 Cor 12. The bible clearly states a new mindset is first and foremost.

The next step to renew your mind is to replace your old thoughts with new thoughts. If you sincerely want to change your life, you will need to develop a schedule and set aside time specifically for the purpose of self-work. You may need to read affirmations, use positive self-talk, looking at motivational/inspirational videos, repeatedly until you look forward to your quality time, all these may be necessary. Now, this scheduled time will look different for everyone. So be comfortable with a schedule that you know you can commit to. Just as it takes a horse twelve months and a woman nine months, to give birth, there is a time and season for all things. During this time, something wonderful within is taking place. With all the affirmations, quiet times in secret, mantras, and other tools used to help develop a new mindset, change is occurring. If you persevere and be disciplined in setting time aside each day, change is automatic. I can say this, because I have experienced change in my life due to my commitment and determination to become the best version of ME, and having this mindset, I KNOW change will continue to occur.

One of the challenges I faced was having very limited space to work and very limited privacy. So, I had to be creative. My creativity depended on my commitment to accomplish what I set out to do. And that is to change my current circumstances and lifestyle to one that is of mutual benefit for ALL. Again, your goal should be aimed toward helping others and you will automatically reach your goals; but this takes time.

There are laws of the Universe that I had never heard of until I began the research for this book. This may be old to some of you but if you're like me, it was new. I have to remind myself of this often.

While combing through all the information available regarding the law of attraction and all the other laws, it's easy to get lost and bombarded with information overload. Key point to remember, consuming too much information at one time will cause brain overload and if you aren't careful, you could easily become frustrated and lose momentum. Always give yourself time to process the information you have consumed and when it's time to move on, you will KNOW.

Remember I mentioned, God spoke these words to me, "Do not seek the golden egg seek the goose that lays the golden egg," which led to Matt 6:33. I am living this scripture at this very moment. Then, back on 1/5/2020, I heard this statement in my spirit, "I am so happy and appreciative now that I have accepted responsibility for my life and all the past choices I made." It was at this time; I made the decision to be held accountable for my life and everything it embraces.

Here's an interesting observation…although I had accepted responsibility for my current state of being, I still did not implement a daily routine. I remember clearly because the coronavirus was clearly a pandemic, and the world was in a state of panic. So much turmoil, anguish, suffering, and yes, torment as well. Now tell me, doesn't this describe HELL? I tell you, we are living in hell every day, when we are separated from unending Communion with God.

As of now, I have come to view life experiences as a movie running on a projector, playing out on the screen of life. And if we are careful, we get to write the script, whether it's a big hit or a flop. We decide!

I embarked on this journey because I needed change in my life. The choices and decisions I made in the past led me to my present state of being. It was time to rely on the power within. So, I began my journey October 2021 with a sincere heart and intent focused on Matt 6:33. So, each day I wake up with the intention of communing with God for new revelations.

Let's talk about the word "decision." Once I heard God speak to me as to where to start my journey, I decided without hesitation, to commit daily to quiet times and journaling. On the surface, we have an idea of what this word means; but do we really understand all that is involved in decision making.

Something happens deep within your being, when you come to a place in life and make a decision regarding your life or other matters of the heart. Decision making should be based on contemplation on the matter at hand as well as consideration of outcomes and the mutual benefit of ALL. I've discovered when designing the life I choose for myself, it is crucial to always work from a place of love for self and humankind.

Changing and/or adding affirmations is a great way to measure progress. If you don't see any noticeable changes in your life, check YOURself and keep affirming. Remember, you will let yourself know when you are being true to yourself and watch what happens.

Write the vision down! Keep it in front of you! This is your dream, your goal, your chief aim in life, whatever resonates with you. When change is occurring, you don't have to say a thing. It will be evident. You will be too busy "being the change" instead of "doing" all the time. When you are changing you are no longer predictable, and you stop talking about everything and expressing opinions on trivial matters, because you are busy just "being". This is a result of developing a habit of spending time alone.

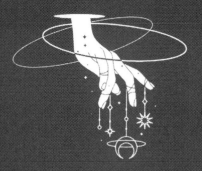

PART IV

DO DUE DILIGENCE

CHAPTER TEN

CAN THIS BE REAL

There are many paths to truth; And I'm sure there are those who'd disagree with me. We in the Western part of the world have a limited mindset when it comes to understanding other religions, cultures, customs, and practices. We tend to close our minds if other worldviews do not line up with what we perceive as true. Americans may sometime even expect others unlike us to forsake cultural practices and customs. Easily said than done. How does one forsake one's culture? Something to think about..

Since the onset of my journey, I have consumed a tremendous amount of information during the past two and a half years and now it's time to reevaluate the knowledge gained from various sources and compare to one of the most well-known books of the world, the Bible. So, today I began to take a closer look at scripture as it relates to this manuscript.

I needed a bible software to aid in bible study and a couple of years ago, Dr. Mike S. Heiser[13] mentioned he uses the logos software for study and research. Dr. Heiser is a renowned author, scholar, and professor of theology. Well today I called Lifeway (Logos) to inquire and to my surprise I learned that Wordsearch software that I purchased years ago was replaced by Lifeway Logos. On the surface,

---

[13] https://drmsh.com/

this does not appear to be significant, but I only *thought* about this software, and God led me to another tool I needed to aid me on this journey. Not only are there various versions and translations of the Bible, but there are other famous Manuscripts as well as other scholarly writings written by the Church Fathers, and many other religious scholars. Logos software is an amazing tool for studying scripture and biblical research. As I begin using Logos, it occurred to me that there must be a way to effect change that will be extremely beneficial to humankind…that is for the mutual benefit of ALL. Then I thought…and thought…and thought. Here is what I had come to experience up to NOW. As you read this chapter and this book, keep in mind this is my life experience based on what I had come to KNOW…and that is MYSELF.

Please understand, I am making no proclamations of anything other than what I found to be true for me. Key here is following the path that leads back to you. Whatever that looks like in your world because you are the creator of your world and staying true to seeking truth, for oneself, will lead back to you. And so, you are sure to find it.

After intense searching and seeking, it all led back to SELF. How amazing is the One we experience as God? I have come to KNOW who I AM, and it is my sincere desire that you gain something from my experience that touches you and inspire you to begin to seek and know for yourself who you are and why you reside in the physical world.

Some of you, if not most, will truly be in awe once you are confronted with your truth. Oprah Winfrey wrote a beautiful piece of art in the form of a book…" What I Know For Sure," that states 'Who you are meant to be evolves from where you are right now' (p 46)." There's that <u>NOW</u> word again! How true is this?

Please be patient with me, I will share how I got to this stage of my life at this moment called NOW. For me, this meant my state of being at this moment, because this is the space that is existing for this moment. And so, my journey was subtly anchored with this KNOWING. Before arriving at the conclusion of the matter, I realized that my journey is now just beginning. On the other hand, as I wrote the last sentence, it occurred to me that my journey isn't just beginning so much as it is a continuation of my journey from the space of <u>KNOWING</u>.

But what I discovered along the way and what I intend to do with the knowledge and truths discerned from this place of KNOWING as it relates to the history of religion and its grip on society, this is the task at hand.

This is what it all comes down to. This is not a decision we leave up to others to take care of…it's up to us, individually and collectively. We must realize <u>who we are</u> and understand <u>our purpose for existence</u>. This is what my journey was all about. I wanted answers to questions that plagued me for years and I didn't find answers from traditional Christianity although some of you disagree with my theology; but nevertheless, <u>IT IS WHAT IS.</u>

Walk with me back to the year 2019 and the month is October. I remember this as though it was yesterday. I was sitting in my bedroom, moving from the bed to my rocking chair, hoping to find some comfort for my aching back. Well, that wasn't all that ached. Remember I said you will receive everything you need along the way? Well, this is what happened to me during the onset of the coronavirus pandemic.

When I came to the realization of certain truths that have been taught since the beginning of organized religion, were not entirely accurate, my heart literally reacted within my chest. For a moment I thought I was having a cardiac infarction of sorts…. I was in so much discomfort, I almost went to the emergency room. I pondered within, what caused this physical reaction in my body, after I realized this truth. And I found it odd, that it was my heart which reacted erratically because of a truth that was unfolding before my very spiritual eyes.

This was the first validation that I was on to something that was causing changes, not only emotionally, but spiritually too. And I had yet to commit to my journey. What I'm about to say may come as a surprise to some but may not surprise others. But, before I reveal the truths that resonated with my soul as true, I need to explain further, revelations I knew to be true. I intend to paint a picture so obvious, you will have no difficulty following, so listen carefully or should I say, pay attention.

Let's begin…before you can move forward, you must know where you are on your journey. I became what I thought was stuck and did not know exactly how to proceed. I came to realize that this was just an illusion, a distraction if I may. What I needed was to step back and put everything that I had consumed and was continuing to consume, in proper perspective. This took time, as I needed to process all this data because somehow, it was ALL connected.

Okay, this is what you've been waiting for! My new truth…. In October 2019, as I mentioned earlier, I experienced pain in my heart when I wrapped my mind around the fact that HELL does not exist in the manner it has been taught and described in the modern Bible we have been using for centuries.

What made me come to this conclusion is my disbelief that God would divvy up Himself for the sake of isolating a portion of Himself to be tormented eternally, and still be pure LOVE and send souls to a place of no return, never returning to from whence they came. The more I thought about this, the more I became concerned and confused. I had to KNOW the truth.

This plagued my mind for several months to no end, until I had this physical experience. Before this experience, my heart was encased in a belief system that the Bible we use today as depicting ALL truths, and nothing else but the truth; and living from this belief system or paradigm my entire adult life, was literally heartbreaking because for me, there was a lack of congruency as I began to examine this well-taught doctrine. Once I realized the truth, I knew this is what I was experiencing. Let me explain. I grew up believing the Bible is the inherent, infallible, perfect Word of God; but I found this not to be so.

The Bible I read and studied all these years lack key information for me to have the ultimate experience that Jesus speaks of throughout the Gospels. And I knew then, something was missing, but I had no concept of how to discover that "something". I could feel that in my soul.

As I continued seeking, I recognized what that "something" is to connect the scriptural dots. I'm not here to attempt to disprove the Bible, or dismiss the truths found therein; that is not my intent; I'm merely pointing out I found the Bible used today, to be incomplete and lacked some of the pertinent information I found relevant in secular and esoteric materials.

Additionally, other noncanonical scrolls I was led to study, were found to be quite useful when studied in conjunction with today's Bible. I compared one of these scrolls with the four canonical gospels, and it is evident that it is congruent in its application. I believe the Bible is one of many sacred texts depicting a path to enlightenment or esoteric wisdom, to aid in finding our way home, back to God. Guess what… we ALL are heading back home to God. Once we no longer desire to live the way we have been, we come to our senses… Study the story of the Prodigal Son.

I yearned to experience the power of God that says, "But as it is written, eye hath not seen, nor ear heard, neither have entered into the heart of man, the things which God hath prepared for them that love him".[14] It was the power of God manifested in scripture, I craved to experience unlike any craving I'd felt before. This is when I realized, my heart was being prepared for what I would encounter later during my journey.

As mentioned earlier, I became so dissatisfied with my current

---

[14] https://www.biblegateway.com/passage/?search=1+Corinthians+2%3A9&version=KJV

state of being and knew I had to do something about that. I struggled within, in the hopes of finding the "Way" that scripture promised.

Then as I began to listen to various videos and audiobooks, I knew there was more to having a deeper understanding of the Universe and the laws which govern it. So, in October 2019, I heard from within, this phrase, "do not seek the golden egg; seek the goose that lays the golden egg." Immediately I knew exactly what this means. Matthew 6:33 came to mind… But seek ye first the kingdom of God, and his righteousness; and all these things shall be added unto you.[15]

Upon hearing these words spoken within, I focused my attention on this scripture. As I stated earlier, I had not fully committed to searching for answers to my questions, at the time. It was more of a haphazard approach…you know, today, maybe tomorrow…you get the idea. But I kept seeking and seeking. Keeping with my timeline, as I meditated on the newfound information, I was at a loss as I had no frame of reference to relate.

Let's back up a moment. August 2019 is when I decided to implement a plan to change my life. So, I began listening to motivational speakers and watching online media discussing the Law of Attraction and affirmations. I had been exposed to this kind of material before; but as I mentioned earlier, because I grew up as a Christian and the thought of such material is considered as New Age and you are doomed to spend eternity in hell. My renewed interest in this area grew and I continued my research into this world of the Law of Attraction and all that is associated with this phenomenon.

As I consumed more and more information about this Law of Attraction, the Law of Vibration, the Law of Cause and Effect…just to name a few, I grew more in tune with what was resonating within. And so, I continued the art of seeking and seeking.

And out of what seemed as nowhere, I heard this from within,

---

[15] https://www.biblegateway.com/passage/?search=Matthew%206%3A3&version=KJV

"God created science (Quantum Theory) for man to discover HIM; And when you find HIM, you will come to experience His Holiness and Awe, even in science". God gives us just a glimpse of how we perceive Him as GOD in our Imagination. This may sound weird, crazy, call it what you want, but I believe GOD is revealed to an individual as one perceives Him to be; hence, the perception of GOD just may be relative in this relative realm. Who has enough knowledge, understanding, and wisdom on this earthly plane, to define God?

CHAPTER ELEVEN

I DON'T BELIEVE YOU, IT CAN'T BE SO

After all the materials and resources, I've sorted through, everything that I encountered along the way makes perfect sense to me now. I ask for wisdom, and I receive wisdom. I am so grateful for this beautiful day. I have a wonderful positive mindset and I choose to feel good. I am grateful for the momentum going forward and being in good spirits and high vibration.

Initially, when I decided I would seek change, I longed to witness the power of God manifested in the Church. Looking back now, I recollect it was sometime in August 2019, I decided to take a different approach to success.

I worked as a licensed insurance agent selling union benefits to anyone who qualified. This was hard work with long dreadful hours. I was eager to develop a system that proved successful and financially rewarding. It was at this time I began listening to various motivational speakers from various walks of life in the hopes of inspiring me to make that big sale.

In hindsight, I realized I had not fully committed to my journey or financial goals and as I'd soon find out, failure to commit with your whole heart will hinder progress; but you get to repeat it again and again, until you get it right. This cycle repeated itself over and over again.

It's now 2020 and the coronavirus is taking its toll on humanity across the globe in pandemic proportions. It seems as though all hope is gone, and the world is in a state unlike anything we've ever seen before. But change is on the horizon, and it will catch on and spread like wildfire. This information cannot be held in once you have EXPERIENCED PURE LOVE flowing throughout your being…you have to share this!

Fast-forward to October 2021, is when I put into place a simple system to spend time alone to find answer to questions, I'd been asking, although not fervently, nearly two years; and now, after finally being fed up with my world, I am ready to hear those answers. I persevered because I knew occasional visits in my quiet times will not be enough. I became intent on my purpose and continued searching and seeking.

And this is when I came to realize we ALL must come together with a common goal to unify this world and try a new and different approach. I believe it was Einstein who said, "We cannot solve our problems with the same thinking we used when we created them."[16]

The challenges we face as a human race cannot be solved by any other means, other than a spiritual approach. And I'm not talking about the organized religions in placed today, that's controlling the masses. I'm talking about each of us going within and begin our journey. I did my research, and one message is consistent and that is, the first step is to spend time in silence and began your search within. We've tried everything else; NOW is always the time to use a new and different approach on a global scale to effect change and turn this world around. There is so much power in unity! And we can do it!

After sifting and sorting through the available resources out there in cyberspace, you can get very confused, misled, or even

---

[16] https://articulous.com.au/problem-solving/#:~:text=%E2%80%9CWe%20cannot%20solve%20our%20problems,created%20them.%E2%80%9D%20Albert%20Einstein.

worse, fail to grasp an understanding as to the importance of living from a place of love, during your journey. It was important for me that I tread these waters lightly. Meaning I struggled with some of the information I came across during my discovery of this new world of what sounded like to me, performing tasks that worked like some form of sorcery or magic.

This all felt so unnatural to me, and I struggled with this for some time; however, there is a silver lining. I was determined to use a proven method to propel me to success. There is only one thing wrong with this way of thinking., my intentions were not necessarily wrong, just a little misguided. But I kept seeking and researching, hoping to find that "magic moment" when everything I touch turn to gold.

What I discovered, the tools I mentioned in the Acknowledgement section, proved useful in developing a routine for me to get in the habit of "putting in the work". You will need time to become familiar with unfamiliar information. And those tools served their purpose well. I would not have been led from one truth to the next without them. Remember, this is a key point.

Everything we need to effect change in our lives, is within, where God resides. Use the tools to aid in discovering truths that resonate with who you really are; and you will KNOW if this is your truth. Always remain true to yourself and you are staying true to God.

You can never deceive yourself, although you think you can deceive others; you can never lie to yourself, but you think you lie to others. To deceive or lie to others, is to deceive and lie to oneself. This bears repeating... always, meaning (continually and in all ways), remain true to yourself and live from that space as you interact with those you encounter; otherwise, you are living from a space that is contrary to who you really are. As a note of caution, when living from your truth, always be mindful of others and how your words may affect them. Living from your truth should be expressed with love and being mindful of others when you find yourself in what may appear to be contradicting.

Now that you have developed a habit of spending time with God, if you have been faithful on your journey, you should have noticed measurable progress. Your thought life should be more focused and when your thoughts stray, you should notice an internal tug, reminding you of your state of being. Once this begins to happen, as long as you keep seeking and seeking, you will come to KNOW who you really are.

Having this KNOWING is the anchor that keeps you in the NOW. When living in the NOW, this is the only time you are NOT living from events from your past (current lifestyle); NOW is the time to focus on, and be mindful of yourself, that is your presence here in this physical world.

Today is just like any other day except for one thing. I had no idea this was the first day of the rest of my life, experiencing a higher level of consciousness. I did not realize what was happening although I was expecting a huge change from the life, I was living just six months ago, dating back to sometime in August of 2021.

For the past several days I have been intently facing inward. During my intent focus within contemplating on God, I experienced a glimpse of what it felt like to be embraced by the power of GOD. This embrace also emanated LOVE, JOY, THANKFULNESS, ABUNDANCE, EVERYTHING. Father showed me an image of the earth appearing in what I call ethereal form, but visible to the naked eye. This was revealed when I recognized that GOD is ALL in ALL and through ALL and I could feel the energy of LOVE. By your words you are justified; by your words you are condemned. Remember this!

Because of the times we are living in today, we must consider, perhaps it's time for a new approach to life and its challenges. We attend various spiritual edifices to give homage to the ONE we recognize as the Creator of ALL things. And yet, when we relate to that ONE, we lose sight of the fact, that ONE is ALL there IS and is IN ALL and through ALL.

This is evident when we tend to attribute events taking place in the world from the perspective of believing that God has a role in that event, one way or the other. I AM here to tell you that in this physical realm…. GOD IS NEUTRAL!!! He is the observer of how life is unfolding in this physical realm. He freely gave us that power and authority to subdue the earth. I believe this was not a proclamation of conquering the physical realm on this earth, but the spiritual or relative realm as well. Although God remains neutral, He is always there to assist and produce the outcome we choose.

If you doubt me, I dare you to view LIFE from this perspective and space with a mindset that everything that is occurring on this planet is by the sole creation of ALL OF US as human beings. God takes no credit for any of this creation or the events that takes place. Our planet, this world, our dwelling place, is by our DOING and it will be by our UNDOING (collective awareness) that we UNDO what is not to our pleasing and mutual benefit for ALL.

CHAPTER TWELVE

IT ALL MAKES SENSE NOW

I hope this book was an easy and practical read, as this was my intention. We've all had to contend with battles of some sort; some of which are quite similar or perhaps the same. Nonetheless, we are NOW HERE and within each of us is this lifeforce that sent us here from our eternal abode. Don't stone me! Allow me to share my discovery of this hidden treasure.

Some of you may have wondered about your reason for this life experience. Whether we are aware of it or not, deep down we all are trying to return to whence we came and that is to return to our Creator. We ALL are a part of GOD's Spirit (for lack of a better description), whatever that may appear to be, and His Spirit is Infinite. I visualized this invisible universe as a Matrix. Simply put, a matrix is basically nothing more than a pattern of sorts.

Inside the Matrix is an invisible set of intricate systems that have evolved into a stream of worldly management structures, communication systems, organized religions, political, and social constructs. We all at some point in our lives have connected with at least one of these systems, one way or another, and most if not, all had no choice in the matter.

The first exposure to a social construct that formed your basic belief and value system is based on the family structure. Our parents or caregivers instilled in us the values handed down to them by their parents and forefathers, so forth and so on. Regardless of the validity of those belief and value systems, we as children adopted those same beliefs and lived from that space. And so, we repeat the cycle. We've passed on to generation after generation, those same values, whether faulty or not. We learned from our parents and forefathers of punishment and reward, biases and prejudices, and other pathological behaviors that is eroding away at society. I believe these faulty belief systems and worldviews, are the sins of the fathers, visiting their children for seven generations.

We have forgotten what it feels like to be loved unconditionally by God. Our parents used a reward/punishment system to manage behavior and when things got out of hand, punishment was handed down. And this is how we relate to God the majority of the time. When a law has been violated or a sin is committed, we fear God and await punishment for that transgression or for missing the mark.

We have believed for so long, that if we fail to obey God's laws or live according to standards set by others, in the name of religion, we will burn in a lake of fire. But if you think about this, what would be the purpose? What would God get out of tormenting his children, a part of Himself? Remember, He created us for His good pleasure.

Can you see all absurdities we have attached to the God of organized religion? Seek God for yourself and pose these questions to Him directly. As I lay in bed before rising, I find myself repeating my affirmation and giving thanks just to be here to give thanks, expecting God to continue to speak and reveal Himself to me. We cannot attempt to label God because when we do, He appears as something different; but His children KNOW His voice.

We have been deceived and lolled to sleep and are now sleep-living. Talk about the living and walking dead! It's time to wake up people! The problem is that you don't know that you are asleep. Jesus spoke on this in the NT, and I will expound on this in more detail later in this chapter.

A lot of you may feel that this is completely off the grid and missing the mark by a long shot; but I will attempt to verify everything I'm saying with scripture. Because I do believe in the Word of God; however, my approach is now different because I have a different mindset.

Growing up as a child and during my adult years, I read and studied the Bible frequently; however, I lacked understanding and wisdom. I did as most of us, attended various churches and found fault with every single one. And so did most of you! But I did not give up. I continued seeking and seeking for truth because the biblical teachings I was exposed to miss the mark for me.

I have always believed something was missing from Scripture in the Western Bible we use today, and the way scripture was being taught, appeared fragmented. With this new mindset, my focus shifted to the ancient ways of old. The subject matter is that "scary" word that most Christians are afraid to speak let alone study and research for oneself. That word is "mysticism". Again, I continue to seek truth and information to validate that truth. I was led to Theodore Nottingham (Gospel of Thomas), an Orthodox Jewish Teacher who solidified my decision to embrace my newfound mindset. You can find this video on YouTube.

This was my first exposure to hearing the Gospel of Thomas.[17] This video was very enlightening and touched me deeply within my being. I suggest viewing this video with an open heart and use this text as a complement to the canonized gospels and see how the power of God is manifested. Truly an amazing experience. But you must approach this knowledge with an open heart.

Having embraced Christianity all my life, this was a very agonizing and painful change of mindset. Viewing Almighty God

---

[17] https://www.pbs.org/wgbh/pages/frontline/shows/religion/maps/primary/gthomas.html

by any other name, other than GOD was blasphemous to me. It was during this time that I came to KNOW God and Jesus as the primordial light in the beginning according to Genesis 1.

Again, I felt that familiar struggle rising within as I wrapped my head around this mystical information that would eventually elevate my understanding to an even higher level of consciousness. To view God the same as Universe, The Light, Source, Infinite Intelligence, and on and on, was disturbing and I dare not believe what I have come to KNOW is sound information and is of God! I struggled for months grasping this ideology as part of the truth I was seeking and was led to, so that I may EXPERIENCE this truth for myself.

To sum up my journey experience up to this point, goes something like this…. I lived my entire life believing everything in the Bible is the infallible word of God and the truths found therein are not to be disputed; however, I found the New Testament to be incomplete and lack certain cohesiveness to experience a part of the Absolute Realm or at least get a glimpse. I won't get into the dogma or theology written within the Bible because that's not my intention.

What I have come to understand, the Bible does contain the Word of God; however, there were other codices that were discarded as trash basically and subsequently defamed and burned because of the unpublicized truths found within these sacred scrolls. Now if the codices we know today are considered canonized as the Holy Scriptures (Bible) and is the Word of God, by whose or what authority were the other codices found useless and fail to meet the criteria to be canonized? The short answer to this question is to maintain control over the masses by way of Religion. Including the logia scribed in the Gospel of Thomas, was evident to the Emperor if the masses interpreted this gospel, he could no longer control their way of thinking or control the Nicaean Council.

They all were supposed to be the Word of God. Instead, the decision boiled down to a simple matter of selecting the most read Scriptures and disposing of the rest, labeling them as forbidden and heretical. Despite the Gospel of Thomas being among those read most often, along with the other well-known scriptures, these codices were purposely omitted from the Judeo-Christian Bible we use today.

Those same codices were deemed as heretical or heresy[18] and anyone caught teaching the messages contained in these scrolls, were put to death, all in the name of God. I wondered what was written in those scrolls and why were they not included as part of the canonized Holy Scriptures used in most churches today?

And the most mysterious question of all, why are some of these old manuscripts are being uncovered now? The unearthing of the Gospel of Thomas dates back to 1945, when a most remarkable find was discovered in Nag Hammadi, Egypt. I reckoned to myself, there is a time and season for all things, and I believe these manuscripts were hidden away for us to study and KNOW ourselves for this age, this season, and this space of time.

The Gospel of Thomas is one of at least forty-five manuscripts that were stored in a clay jar found in Egypt. This gospel was also omitted from the Bible during the reign of Emperor Constantine, around 325 A.D. According to historians, a decision had to be made as to which sacred scrolls should be included in the Judeo-Christian Bible. The emperor appointed Eusebius[19] the task of selecting which scrolls to be included in the canonized Bible for the known Roman Empire (Catholic Church, Political Platform, and Military). This decision led to what we know is the Bible of today with all its various translation.

Now please pay close attention and stay with me. The Gospel of Thomas codices were found in a clay jar, buried beneath the sands of time. A fragment of this manuscript was found earlier in 1849, and later revealed as part of the heading "Gospel of Thomas". This new discovery in Nag Hammadi, Egypt in 1945 is causing a stir as these texts relates to Jesus and how we commune with God.

---

[18] https://www.britannica.com/topic/heresy
[19] https://www.britannica.com/biography/Eusebius-of-Caesarea

This book, the Gospel of Thomas is considered to be the words spoken by Jesus to the masses and privately to his disciples. You can find a free copy of this text online and read it for yourself and compare it with the four Gospels. You will find the Gospel of Thomas complements the other gospels, unquestionably. These sayings were written down by one of Jesus' disciples, Thomas the Twin.

When I first encountered this gospel, it set me on a course that propelled me to another level of awareness; far beyond what I'd imagined. And you may have a similar experience. I just know these sayings are filled with the power of God. Jesus demonstrated that power and authority in the flesh. He is a perfect example of divinity in the flesh, and we are to be just as He is. It is written throughout the canonized gospels and in the Gospel of Thomas. Once we drink of Jesus's cup, we are as he is. Read it for yourself. We are One with the Father, God.

My reasoning behind this theory is based on the content found within some of these manuscripts which is applicable to the uncertainties we are confronted with today on a global scale. These manuscripts contain revelations of enormous proportions and is baffling to religious professors, theologians, historians, physicists (quantum, experimental, and theoretical), and philosophers, just to mention a few, stretching from one end of the world to the next. This one mere fact, should speak to you on some level, <u>screaming something is wrong with the state of this world and our state of being</u>. The old system, <u>organized religion</u> is no longer working, and the world is now in a state worse than ever before. It's time to step back and re-member who we really are.

You may ask by whose authority I say what I say, and my answer to you is I qualify because I am humankind just as you are. And not only do I have authority; but so do you, and I strongly suggest that we exercise that authority NOW. The question to ask if you haven't already, "how do we do that?". And that is a legitimate question, however, you need a crash course in understanding one among many other sacred texts found in Nag Hammadi in 1945. Dr. Elaine Pagels has completed extensive research on the Gnostic Gospels and has written numerous groundbreaking books regarding her research.[20] There are plenty other credible sources available online to study for yourself.

This journey is planned by <u>designed</u> instead of <u>default</u> once you realize you are a spiritual entity, that lives in a body, encased by your soul, having an earthly experience. When you understand and embrace this concept, focus on finding your highest truth about yourself. Once you know that and experience that truth, you are free.

Discover your truth for yourself and you decide. After immersing myself in the Gospel of Thomas, I found Dr. Pagels' online channel on YouTube. I stumble upon this information during my journey after discovering spiritual teaching that recently grew the attention of a wide range of subject matter experts. Keep in mind, I have been on my journey almost two years and I continue seeking to ensure I understand new information that is brought to me.

I think in terms of logic, and I always look to more than one source to verify what is heartfelt. And it is important that I find credible sources to validate what resonates with me on my journey. This is very personal and yet I feel the need to share my experience.

After studying the books written by Dr. Pagels, I had come to a fork in the road again, so to speak, and was unsure as to which path to take in completing my book. I did, however, continue to listen to inspiring and motivating videos to maintain a level flow of energy instead of allowing this momentary delay to zap me of flowing positive energy. Father knew my heartfelt prayer and desire and He allowed me to experience Love, Joy, Thanksgiving, Humility, and Assurance.

This led to how I discovered other spiritual teachings and ultimately more credible sources to validate my experiences, to

---

[20] https://religion.princeton.edu/people/faculty/core-faculty/elaine-pagels/

appeal to my analytical mind. Father knew I needed this kind of information to settle any doubts I possessed, once and for all.

I think this is my third or fourth EXPERIENCE of feeling an intense vibration of God's energy of pure love and each time, it appears to be more intense than the last experience. The truths most people hold close to their hearts, are rooted in organized religion and the teachings that were and are being taught, are not from a place of pure love; these truths are based on what others have said God told them and they told others and so forth and so on.

To me, this serves as no better interpretation than mine. Religious institutions and churches have a vested interest in how one thinks. If one can tell someone what to think, then the mind can be trained to accept what is being taught as the truth, whether it's a lie or is of no consequence. It literally does not make any difference.

Everything we've heard about God is contradictory to say the least. We say God is Love; but we kill in the name of God and expect a great reward in the afterlife. What kind of God is this? This sounds more like the devil if there was such an entity. If God is ALL there IS, then God is in everything that we encounter; the good and the evil; the up and the down; the right and the wrong, the joy and the sadness. To know God is to know the AM NOT-NESS of God too.

We are taught that God is the Great I AM, the Great Unseen…. We focus on the I AM-NESS of God and ignore the I AM NOT-NESS of God…folks, this is ALL GOD…. get it? We have compartmentalized God and place Him is a particular realm outside of ourselves. But this is literally impossible because God can't NOT be in and through us because again, HE IS ALL THERE IS.

A new EXPERIENCE of the God of old is NOW HERE. We can no longer relate to God as we have done in the past up to this day. This is the same God that existed in the days of old and is the same God today. To understand and relate to God today, requires one to stop and take a mental inventory of the state of not only our country, but the entire world. Something must change … the God of the days of old must be experienced in such a way that speaks to the multitudes today. We must be opened to understand how God communicates with us individually, and collectively as one body.

Now that I have a fundamental understanding of communion with God, I began to study the Gospel of Thomas alongside the synoptic (overview) gospels in the Judeo-Christian Bible we use today. The Gospel of Thomas is unlike the other gospels, however, there are many similarities that can be found in the synoptic gospels. And this is the focus of the remaining portion of this chapter I chose to end this book.

In an effort to complement the Gospels I came to rely on throughout my life, I pondered each sayings of the Gospel of Thomas and immediately, I could feel God's Presence in and around me. I will attempt to share with you what I EXPERIENCED, after reading and meditating on some of these sayings, as it relates to this book up to now.

The Gospel of Thomas begins by stating these are the secret sayings spoken by the living Jesus Himself, that were recorded by Didymos Judas Thomas, believed to be one the Twelve Disciples. Just to remind you which disciple this text is speaking of, you remember the disciple referred to as "Doubting Thomas". It's no coincidence, this disciple is labeled as such because of the fact Jesus spoke profound teachings privily to the disciples and Thomas in particular. There is a reference to this saying in the manuscript (Logion 13).

This chapter is not an overview of this gospel; however, as I go through the book, certain logia will be referenced as I explain its impact on me during my EXPERIENCES. I will quote the sayings, then expound on its impact. Unfortunately, I cannot expound on each one as this is not the present focus. God has already spoken there will be a second book based on this theology.

"1 And he said, "Whoever discovers the interpretation of these sayings will not taste death" (See footnote 16).

When I first read this saying, I was a little bewildered until I had my first EXPERIENCE. Suddenly, everything became so clear, simple, and plain. These are the words that immediately came to me.

My mind immediately thought of Elijah, who is said to have not tasted death and was carried up in a whirlwind which was GOD's way of saying you have fulfilled your purpose (played your role/ done what you came to Earth to do) and now it's time for your next role. I believe LIFE is just this simple but by no means easy-peasy. It takes *daily* practice to live your life on purpose. I know many of you may think differently and that is absolutely okay. You will think, act, and be (live) from the space you live from day in and day out, and this is your right.

There have been occasions during quiet times of retrospect, I felt as though my body was literally, for lack of a better description, becoming a mass of waves and vibration, and yet I was totally aware of what was happening. In the center of this EXPERIENCE, I sensed reverence, wonderment, and a feeling of undeniable PURE LOVE. I did not depart as Elijah did; but I felt as though I could. Now, death holds an entirely different meaning for me. I comprehend what it means to be absent from the body is to be present with the Lord and you don't have to die to have this EXPERIENCE.

You read in a previous chapter, GOD led me to begin my journey by studying Matthew 6:33 and this was the beginning of my awareness of who I really AM. Please pay close attention and notice how God used scripture to guide me to the Gospel of Thomas, a noncanonical scroll to complement my journey.

Amazingly enough, the Gospel of Thomas opens with answering Matthew 6:33, seek ye first…. And goes on to explain what I will encounter when I seek and continue seeking. We never cease to seek and seek. And so, this leads to the next two sayings of Jesus, written down by Thomas...

> "2 Jesus said, "Those who seek should not stop seeking until they find. When they find, they will be disturbed. When they are disturbed, they will marvel, and will rule over all."
>
> 3 Jesus said, "If your leaders say to you, 'Look, the (Father's) imperial rule is in the sky,' then the birds of the sky will precede you. If they say to you, 'It is in the sea,' then the fish will precede you. Rather, the (Father's) imperial rule is inside you and outside you. When you know yourselves, then you will be known, and you will understand that you are children of the living Father. But if you do not know yourselves, then you live in poverty, and you are the poverty" (See footnote 16).

These sayings resonated so profoundly with whom I somehow knew, I already AM. But how can one KNOW this for sure? As I have stated so many times throughout the pages of this book, you have to open up and prepare your heart to realize your truth. And to do this, one must enter into their secret closet, lock the door, and sup with HIM. You will find no better dining in all the world or in space for that matter.

Now, allow me to talk about logion two. According to this saying ..."Those who seek should not stop seeking until they find. When they find, they will be disturbed. When they are disturbed, they will marvel, and will rule over all." What an amazing saying because this is exactly what happened to me.

I clearly understand NOW why God led me to begin with Matthew 6:33...Seek ye first the kingdom of God .... God knew how this gospel would impact my journey; thus opening my heart up even more. This was clearly God letting me know that the journey begins with seeking and seeking; and so, this is what I did, and as stated previously, I found a truth that resonates with everything within my beingness. This led me to the next truth, which too resonated with me and so forth and so on, up to my current state of being.

Here's what's interesting about seeking and seeking. Notice in this saying, when you seek, there is no doubt that you are going to find that which you are seeking and once you find that truth, this knowledge, this truth will be very disturbing to you because it's like nothing you have ever read or been taught in organized religion. This truth is so literally "out of this world", one may think this is unbelievable and can't be of God. This new aspect of God is not the familiar way we are accustomed to labelling or relating to God; and so, we choose to believe that this seems unlike the God we thought we knew and discount the experience as nothing more than a fluke.

But I accepted this saying as a truth that resonated with me. I was astonished at this amazing truth. Because now that I have a deeper conceptualization of who I really AM, I have a better understanding as to how to overcome life's adversities and spread the Gospel of the Good News...sharing with everyone who they really are.

When you KNOW your true identity, and EXPERIENCE this KNOWING, you can and will rule over ALL...that is YOUR being. Ruling over the ALL is evitable because you are NOW living and EXPERIENCING LIFE from a new perspective and mindset, recognizing that we are ALL connected, many members in One Body.

Logion three explains about the kingdom of God and where it is located. The Gospel of Thomas makes it perfectly clear that the Kingdom of God in wherever God IS...inside, outside, and all around each of us; but the only way to see the Kingdom of

God according to this saying, is summed up as this... "When you know yourselves, then you will be known, and you will understand that you are children of the living Father. But if you do not know yourselves, then you live in poverty, and you are the poverty" (See footnote 16).

What else do you need to understand that the key to this LIFE is to KNOW ourselves and the only way to KNOW ourselves is to go within and enter into our secret closet, lock the door behind us and get to know in secret who we really are. When I first read these first two sayings, I KNEW beyond any shadow of doubt, that when I found myself, I found GOD.

This is a fact! Otherwise, failing to know oneself, that is spending time seeking and seeking during quiet times, will cause one to create life by default instead of by design. If one continues doing what one always does, one will continue being, doing, and having the same state of being repeatedly. It's time to stop living your past over and over again.

ABOUT THE AUTHOR

Elle grew up in a small town in rural Mississippi, raised by her widowed grandmother who is now deceased. At the time of Elle's mother's untimely death, she and her siblings were separated and placed with both paternal and maternal grandparents. Elle was only five years old, and she and her younger brother were immediately placed in an environment that would ultimately guide her to a path that is continuing to manifest itself in ways that are truly astonishing.

She attended Nugent Center High School in Benoit, MS and graduated at age 16, top of her class in 1975, earning full academic scholarship to Alcorn State University, Lorman, MS. One of the most fulfilling accomplishments during her high school achievements was being one of those chosen students of Whos' Who Among American High School Students' annals.

Additionally, during Elle's high school years, she became very active in sports and other scholastic activities. She enjoyed basketball especially and was quite a skillful player. The school she attended was a very close and personal experience as the principal, teachers, and other staff members ensured the educational needs were met as well as a safe place for children to grow and flourish. The staff and teachers were entrusted with preparing students for the world of life experiences. And did so to the best of their abilities.

After graduating from high school, Elle attended Alcorn State

University and was recruited to participate in the Agricultural Department. After completing her Sophomore year at Alcorn State University, she decided to leave school for a while. Ultimately, Elle graduated from Dallas Baptist University, earning a BAS in Psychology and Biblical Studies, August 2005.

Printed in the United States
by Baker & Taylor Publisher Services